Photographing the
World

A guide to photographing 201 of
the most beautiful places on Earth

Tom Till

PHOTOGRAPHING THE WORLD
A Guide to 201 of the most beautiful places on Earth

Published by PhotoTripUSA Publishing™
An imprint of

GRAPHIE
INTERNATIONAL, INC.
8780 19th Street, Suite 199
Alta Loma, CA 91701, USA

Text & photography Copyright © 2012 by Tom Till

Executive Editor & Publisher: Laurent Martrès

Book Design: Sioux Bally-Maloof, Heartstone Arts

Copy Editor: John Stottlemyer

Cover photo: Machu Picchu, Peru
Title page photo: Angel Falls, Venezuela

Additional photography: Sossusvlei aerial p.28, Dead Vlei p.29, Petra p.48, Machapuchare p.63, Annapurna p.64, Amalfi p.151, Positano p.152, Tuscany p.155, Varenna p.158, Portofino p.159, Monet's Garden p.171, Annecy p.174, Burano p.183, Lake Bled p.185 top, Reine p.192, Moraine Lake p.276, Lake Maligne p.276, Peyto Lake p.277, Llama p.310b, Laguna Verde p.313, Arbol de Piedra p.313, Isla Incahuasi p.314, Parinacota p.314, Lago Pehoe p.319 © Laurent Martrès; Seychelles p.38 © Leksele; Bromo p.79 © Ijansempoi; Borobudur p.80 © Luciano Mortula

Printed in China

Important notice: Some of the locations described in this book require travel through remote areas, which may not always be safe. Travel at your own risk and always check conditions locally before venturing out. The author and publisher decline all responsibility if you get lost, stranded, injured, or otherwise suffer any kind of mishap as a result of following the advice and descriptions in this book. Furthermore, the information contained herein may have become outdated by the time you read it; the author and publisher assume no responsibility for outdated information, errors, and omissions.

Publisher's Cataloging-in-Publication

    Till, Tom.
        Photographing the World : a guide to 201 of the most
    beautiful places on Earth / Tom Till.
        p. cm.
        ISBN 9780916189228

        1. Travel photography. 2. Travel--Guidebooks.
    I. Title.

    TR790.T55 2012   778.9'9
                    QBI12-600119

INTRODUCTION

Preamble

This may surprise you, but I did not own a passport until I was almost forty years old. Unlike some of my more fortunate college friends, visiting Europe was as likely for me as acquiring front row tickets to a Rolling Stones concert. Besides, I had the Western United States as a playground, and in particular the Colorado Plateau. I moved there as a young man and took up photography. While in my twenties, I happened to see a catalog from the fledgling outdoor travel company, Mountain Travel, and it opened my eyes to some of the world's wonders outside America. From the money I was making as a teacher and aspiring photographer, I could only visit such a place by plunking down a year's salary for a single trip. At that time, traveling to a far-away destination like I saw in the catalog resided in my psyche as a dream that could never be fulfilled.

After spending decades photographing within the borders of the United States, I received a huge windfall when a client lost a large number of my photos that were on loan to him. At that point, I decided to lug my 4x5 camera overseas to try and capture some imagery that American landscape photographers had not, as yet, turned their attention to. Since few photographers were selling large format stock imagery of the places I visited—Ireland, New Zealand, Costa Rica, Australia, and Chile among them—my plan worked very well. I was able to sell the large format images as stock photography and pay for all my trips, enjoying a profit besides.

After 25 years of this, it dawned on me that I had unique knowledge and expertise that few individuals possess: good strategies borne from on-the-ground experience about how to photograph the world's most beautiful landscapes. This is combined with a background understanding of these destinations, where they are located, and the best time to be there.

What this book is not

This book is not a travel guide; it is first and foremost a photography book. If you want information on how to get to the places listed herein, travel logistics, and where to stay and eat once you arrive, you can easily find it elsewhere. If you're concerned about security and your health, as you should be, that information is also available from other sources. This world changes so rapidly that some places listed here may be perfectly safe today, but could become dangerous tomorrow. Weighing these considerations is not covered within this volume.

If you are looking for a book about the specifics of photographing wildlife, this book is also not really for you. Though you may encounter wildlife visiting the landscapes I profile, it will likely be serendipitous.

Scope of this Book

The book briefly describes 201 of the world's most majestic landscapes and gives first-hand information about how, when, and where to photograph them. Many entries are from famous places that every landscape photographer—and even non-photographers—will know. Many others are places that you may have never heard of. Some are huge areas like the Amazon, while others, like Mesa Arch in Utah, allow room for only a few photographers at one time. Site selection for the book was left to me, and reflects my interests and passions, since I needed to personally visit and photograph each locale. My entire career has been a series of self-assignments. Since I was not funded by any one source, I had complete freedom to photograph where I pleased. Conversely, since I didn't have a deep-pocketed publisher paying the bill, almost every destination in this book has at least a modest infrastructure, and you will not have to mount an expedition to get there.

I personally know most of the successful landscape photographers of the baby-boom generation, and a few who are younger. The sites listed here reflect the subjects generally of interest to the majority of professional photographers like us. They include mountains, deserts, lakes, rivers, oceans, wetlands, forests, archeological sites, cityscapes, and tourist attractions. More specifically, landscape photographers are drawn to wildflower blooms, waterfalls, rock formations, interesting weather, plants and trees, reflections, ancient and historical structures, and seasonal changes. You will find all these represented in the book.

I know many people will disagree with my selections. Some may be debatable while many are not. This book could easily have covered 251 locations, and the next edition may do so. I tried to include as many countries as possible, and in doing so may have lowered my standards a little to include a representative location. I will also admit that some of the largest countries in size: Canada, Russia, Brazil, and China are underrepresented for the scenic treasure they have. I could have compiled an entire book for each of these countries.

You will find a number of ancient monuments represented in the book. I started out strictly as a nature photographer, but found out years ago that I got as much of a kick from shooting the pyramids as I did Yosemite National Park. Also, I'm a desert guy. I live in the desert and I love the light and the subjects found there. Since I prefer to shoot with more sun and less cloud, deserts work best for that too. There are fewer people around and it's usually really clean. Mountains, and in particular the Himalayas, are not as well represented in this book as they probably should be. I'll admit that. The reason I've made two trips to that mountain range and 14 to the deserts of Australia is love of dry wastes and a life-long problem with altitude sickness. Also, I've spent a great deal of time in some of the world's most beautiful mountains waiting out fog that never cleared, or watching clouds that obscured peaks for weeks at a time. No one ever feels sorry for me, but I guess they have a point.

My hope is that this book will also find a broader audience than just photographers. If you are a traveler with just a modest interest in photography, you can be sure you will experience the world's finest scenic wonders by visiting the places I suggest. Photographers know the most alluring locations and spend a great deal of time and energy searching them out.

An aid to planning

The purpose of this book is to help you plan and execute better photographs than you could on your own, and with less time and money spent in the process. It has become prohibitively expensive for serious photographers to turn up at a random location, at a random time of year, and expect to come away with good images. This is even more the case when traveling to far-flung locations around the globe. Paradoxically, breathtaking scenic locales are not always easy to photograph. First, the very grandeur you're trying to capture may overwhelm you so that you are almost afraid to begin. Furthermore, there's the challenge to do something new with an over-photographed subject, though many photographers are quite happy with a good scene that mimics the results of thousands of others. I try to help you here, by offering some suggestions about opportunities for images that the locale may provide. One of my strategies is to visit a place and visualize how it will look at different times of the year in terms of weather, sun angle, the moon, and dozens of other factors. Many entries talk about these possibilities, especially the under-appreciated importance of sun angle. I offer suggestions about the best times of the year to visit, which lenses to use, and when HDR (High Dynamic Range), a GND (Graduated Neutral Density) filter, or other post-production techniques may be helpful. I will use these acronyms exclusively throughout the book. A planning aid I use frequently is The Photographer's Ephemeris. This amazing app provides sunrise, sunset, moonrise and moonset times overlaid with map information for any location in the world. It's worth its weight in gold, and should be on your tablet, as soon as possible.

A note about security

Though some anthropologists insist the modern world is a less dangerous place now than in the past, it certainly seems to be pretty scary out there at times. Last year for example, I missed the Libyan war by two weeks, the Japanese earthquake by one day, and was scheduled to be on the cruise ship that was stuck in the Indian Ocean. Luck, good and bad, is certainly a factor in photography and travel. I have visited all the places described in the book and personally experienced only one non-violent robbery plus an attempt to be flagged down in South Africa, a disguised robbery attempt, I'm certain. Beyond that, no one has even spoken a harsh word to me, although I did make some Italian drivers very mad when I went through a tunnel at only the posted speed limit. I mind my manners, follow the golden rule, keep a low profile and don't frequent bars at night.

Also keep in mind that rural areas, where you'll do most of your shooting, are usually safer than cities. I also believe skimping on lodging is a mistake. You will want to stay in the best places you can afford, which are usually the most secure, both crime and health-wise. And they are the best places to be if you need help. Traveling in a group with a reputable tour company is also safer than traveling alone. Traveling alone is usually the best way to go for photography purposes, but consider hiring guides and drivers to help you.

I have found cruises to be one of the safest and least expensive ways to visit a number of great photography locales in the course of a week or two, even with the bad press they have recently received. My last cruise visited the Cayman Islands, Honduras, Belize, and other places in the Western Caribbean. If I'd flown to each locale separately, the cost of flights and the time incurred would have been prohibitive. I didn't have to make lodging or meal arrangements, and my personal effects including my camera, were always safe. Frequently, the ships stay in port past the magic hour, giving you the chance to shoot at sunset.

Probably the biggest danger while traveling would be the danger you face at home: some kind of vehicle accident. Acts of terrorism, kidnapping, or airplane crashes are statistically insignificant when compared to car accidents. Ultimately, your security rests upon your shoulders. None of the places in this book are risk-free, and some at times may be downright dangerous. Read U.S. State Department Consular sheets in advance for any country you hope to visit, and check with the CDC (Center for Disease Control) and other sources about disease dangers. Do yourself a huge favor and get the appropriate inoculations when recommended. Staying safe is completely your responsibility, so please take it seriously. I have, and it has worked for me. My hope is that your travels will be as trouble-free as my own.

Problems at customs & in the field

I've never heard of a photographer being turned around at customs because they had excessive "professional" equipment. I won't say it can't happen, however. I have had some issues flying into Canada, the United Kingdom, Micronesia, Japan, and Ireland, but after a brief delay I was told to go on my merry way. Elsewhere in this book, I mention some of the troubles I've had while shooting with my 4x5 and tripod, primarily at archeological sites. I recently heard that Lower Antelope Canyon—an Arizona slot canyon—now has signs saying that no pictures taken there can be used even on Facebook without permission. Facebook seems to be the new obsession with those who want to control photographers. People always ask me, "Why do they want to stop you from shooting?" I don't have an answer, and most of the time it seems to me like bureaucratic nonsense. On the island of Dominica recently, for example, the authorities told me I couldn't use my tripod because they thought I was shooting for the "cruise ship".

My question is, in a country with 60 percent unemployment, why would they care even if I were promoting the island's natural wonders for the cruise ship? Eventually I talked my way in, which you may be able to do also. In India, at least half the places I visited did not allow tripods, and there was never any real rhyme or reason why one site was tolerant and one wasn't. Greece and Mexico have to take the prizes for being the most uncooperative places for photographers, especially at archeological sites. One would think that with the trouble Greece is in, it would welcome any visitor, but it's not the case. Fortunately, technology has provided a solution to this problem with new generations of IS and VR lenses that allow us to shoot at slower shutter speeds without a tripod. Also, boosting the ISO setting can mitigate this issue.

If tripods are not allowed at a given location, I do say so. If there is no such mention, one should assume they are allowed.

What about equipment?

Most of the images in the book were taken with a heavy and difficult to use 4x5 camera. This was the tool of choice for most professional landscape photographers in the United States before the digital age. The camera produced a transparency 4x5 inches in size, required a kit that weighed in at almost fifty pounds, and drew attention from anyone who encountered it. In all, I used the 4x5 in almost 80 countries and all fifty states. Obviously, this format is not recommended now, and I switched to 35mm digital in 2008. I have used both Canons and Nikons, usually with the highest megapixel count available at the time. Most non-professionals will not want to purchase such a sophisticated camera, but landscape photographers are fans of detail and go to great lengths to get it. With lenses, I try to cover as much of the spectrum as I can, and with the Canon I have a fisheye, and zooms that range from 8mm to 400mm. I carry a spare small sensor body for emergencies and it allows me to convert my 400mm lens to a 600mm lens due to the "crop factor". I shoot with a tripod whenever possible, and I am a fan of the Really Right Stuff ball heads and tripods. In the workshops I teach, I see a resistance to using tripods generally, and those who do use one seldom acquire a good tripod. A quality tripod can increase the integrity of your images more than just about anything you do, so I strongly suggest you secure a good one and use it whenever possible. Make sure your camera has the live view function, which has revolutionized focusing in landscape photography. With the capability to focus in "real depth of field," live view allows you to focus at the right place in the scene to maximize sharpness, and for infinity shots to be focused right on the money every time.

I carry my camera gear on to the plane, and by using my credit card to reach elite status I can board the plane first and always find a place for my camera bag. Most times I check my large heavy tripod although this has lead to problems on a few occasions when my luggage has been delayed. I have never had anything stolen from my luggage, although the TSA did destroy a new 4x5 camera in my checked luggage (after 9-11, my 4x5 gear was too big to be allowed for carry-on) when an agent tried to penetrate its secrets with a screwdriver. Digital photography has made most of the problems I dealt with for decades go away, especially the problem of carrying sheet film with me. I was really lucky that no one ever demanded I open one of my boxes of exposed film in the hundreds of security checks I have been through. If you are still using film, I can tell you that with low ISO film, and even with a dozen or more trips of running 4x5 film through the scanners, I never noticed any problems with my images from airport x-ray machines.

Always make sure you have plenty of flash cards and watch your battery levels carefully, especially when using live view. Once a card has images, I treat it as the most important piece of property I have besides my passport. I carry some small drives—they only weigh seven ounces and are 4x3 inches in size—and download my images to those as a backup, but I don't erase any cards until I've safely uploaded them to my computer at home. As an additional precaution, I carry the cards and the drives in two different places while traveling.

Aerial photography

Several of the sites listed here can be photographed most effectively by shooting from a light plane, helicopter, or balloon. Many scenic hot spots are offering visitors a chance to easily book a tour in one of these conveyances. In Australia, helicopters are everywhere. Try to book the first or last flight of the day, and if possible try to get the seat with the window. This varies a great deal in helicopters, so talking to the pilots beforehand would be helpful. Most of the other passengers won't care if they have a window as long as they have a good view. Windowless helicopters are preferred, although they are smaller, thus more expensive. I have obtained excellent images through glass on airliners, helicopters, and small fixed-wing aircraft using a polarizing filter. Remember to use at least 1/1000 of a second as your shutter speed with aperture set wide open (i.e., f1.8, f2, f2.8, etc.). Push up your ISO to make sure you can attain these settings on your camera. The same techniques should be used on fixed wing scenic flights. With other passengers on board, the price of these usually short flights can be quite reasonable.

After a surge of popularity 25 years ago, balloon rides can again be found at many spectacular spots around the world. I recently enjoyed a balloon flight at Bagan, and found it to be a great opportunity. Almost all balloon flights launch before dawn, and you will need the same settings mentioned above. If you ascertain which direction the balloon will be going, it will be to your advantage to get a spot on the forward side of the balloon to be shooting towards your subject rather than turning around to shoot where you've already been. A rash of fatal accidents from commercial balloon rides in Cappadocia and New Zealand is an indication that these trips bring with them a degree of risk. Sadly, scenic flights over the Himalayas and in Zion National Park crashed while I was working on this book.

Shooting at night

Digital cameras with highly evolved sensors have revolutionized photography of the nighttime sky, and shooting the many world wonders listed in this book that are illuminated at night is much easier than ever before. A tripod is an absolute necessity for this type of work. Since you'll probably want to use a wide-open aperture, or as wide as possible, pre-focusing on your subject before dark or knowing exactly where to set your focus is important. A fast lens, typically a prime (non-zoom) that opens to at least f1.8, is also very helpful.

Travel and caring about the places you photograph

We cannot gloss over the fact that travel uses up a lot of the Earth's declining resources, but I still believe that its benefits to the traveler as well as to the place the traveler visits can be substantial. If you believe as I do, that global warming is real, carbon offsets, offered now by many airlines, are a great thing to do. Also, the transfer of much needed resources through travel from affluent to developing countries, and the understanding between cultures that takes place is a significant positive move towards a more peaceful, livable world for all. Though a great number of the sites listed here are part of the UNESCO World Heritage Site program, most are vulnerable to damage from outside development, air and water pollution, and in some cases, excessive visitation. Many of the destinations listed here can use your help. Donations to groups like the Nature Conservancy, the NRDC, the Sierra Club, and many others can help ensure that the great wonders of our planet will be around for our children and the world's children to enjoy.

No matter how much reading and preparation for a photography trip you do, it's not always enough. Guides can fill this void and put you in place for great photography, getting you to the best spots at the right time. Sometimes guides completely tuned in to photography can be obtained; at other times, you will be dealing with guides who rarely work with photographers. This is something that should be hashed out while negotiating to hire help. Remember that you are paying the tab, and make sure you can change the program as you see fit. One very important point your guide must understand is that you will likely want to be in the field for sunrise and sunset. With guides unfamiliar with photography, I ask which direction the sun hits a particular subject and at what time. Even if the guide is not a photography specialist, they can usually answer these questions.

In general, I hire guides more often in developing countries. Though most guides are wonderful and experts on their area, you will occasionally run into some ornery individuals. If I'm with a friend, I play bad cop while he plays good. I had a particularly difficult guide in Turkey recently; he kept asking me if I was a "guy," and I always answered yes, not realizing that he was really trying to say "gay," which I'm not (not that there's anything wrong with it). I received a large refund from the tour company for his inappropriate advances.

Snag at Sossusvlei at Sunrise, Namib Dunes

AFRICA

Huge Statues of Ramesses II

Abu Simbel – Egypt

The thrill of being the only person at Abu Simbel at dawn was something I'll never forget. In the clean desert air on a perfectly clear morning, the crimson light on the huge statues carved from solid rock, was as saturated and strong as any I've ever seen. I would assume that most mornings in this part of the Sahara are similar. The stone temples at Abu Simbel were constructed during the reign of Ramesses II in the 13th century BC.

I had photographed some images of the shadowed rock at sunset when I first arrived, but morning was much better. Sunrise is Abu Simbel's photographic moment, and all one needs to do is be there and set up. The standard shot is from directly in front of the facade, but I also climbed up the back of the rock to shoot down from above. This high perspective is also an impressive image.

One person was present at the site in the evening when I arrived who told me to go away and not come back. Fortunately, he was nowhere to be seen at dawn. If there are human impediments keeping you from Abu Simbel at first light, I'm sure some 'baksheesh' payments will help. It's pretty hard to screw this up. The only thing that might slow you down is your jaw dropping as the red light quickly slides down the face of this colossus.

A guide here would be helpful but is not required. Access is by foot or taxi and Abu Simbel is open 24 hours a day, year-round.

Avoid mosquitoes and dogs, which seem to frequent the area. Malaria and rabies are not unknown at this location. Security in Egypt is always a concern.

Luxor – Egypt

At Luxor, both sides of the Nile provide amazing opportunities for photographing ruins of ancient Egypt.

The Karnak complex on the east side of the river is only a short distance from the hotels there. The front walls glow best at sunset with the row of ram sphinxes

Luxor Temple exterior

Ramesses II head and Colossi

along the processional adding to the composition. Inside Karnak, at places like the Hypostyle Hall, sunlight bounces around the hieroglyphic columns not unlike a slot canyon, producing excellent warm light on the sandstone. At other places, the white columns take on a distinctly blue hue with open-shade lighting. One excellent shot is the Ramesses II head at ground level, with surrounding stone and statuary that turns blue, red and purple in the low sunset light. Again, the similarity to shooting in slot canyons with a lot of bounced light is apparent, at least to me. As sunset approaches, move to the west-facing exterior walls with huge columns and ruined statues.

The main outdoor attraction of the west side of the river is the Valley of the Kings, with the unusual Hatshepsut Temple cut into one of the most imposing rock walls in Egypt. This structure is oriented towards sunrise light. To get there in time for dawn, your guide will have to get you up early and drive you to a nearby bridge. By climbing a small hill near the parking lot, you are afforded a tremendous view of the distinctive temple and its surrounding cliffs, glowing red at dawn. You can then ride back on the ferry that operates during daylight hours.

A guide is recommended at Luxor.

Right: Hypostyle Hall columns

Khafre Pyramid and the Great Sphinx in morning fog

The Pyramids & Sphinx – Egypt

The only surviving member of the original seven wonders of the ancient world, the Giza Pyramids are truly awe-inspiring. Even though they've been photographed a great deal, shooting the pyramids is not an easy task. This is true even with a guide, something I recommend heartily. Perhaps I was a prime target, shooting with a 4x5 camera, but I was constantly approached by people demanding to perform unwanted tasks for me and expecting to get paid. Also, I was told that just walking around the area of the pyramids was not allowed and I had to ride a camel. This was a horrible experience.

Obviously, this is a location that would be much more comfortable in winter, and when I was there fog appeared every morning. The mist added a great element of

Pyramids of Khufu, Khafre & Menkaure

mystery to both the pyramids and the sphinx. In the winter, the Sphinx is a morning shot, while the pyramids look best from the west at sunset and are spectacular with a medium focal-length lens. It's quite easy in the morning to line up the Sphinx with the pyramids beyond. I didn't have any clouds during the week I was there, but you may be more fortunate, as clouds would certainly add a lot of drama to the scene. Since traveling through Cairo is very difficult, select lodging as close to the pyramids as you can.

A guide is recommended here. Permits are not required and tripods are allowed.

Leptis Magna – Libya

Instead of being covered with cinders and lava like Pompeii, Leptis Magna— the remains of the largest Roman city in Africa—was covered with sand for almost a millennium, providing one of the best-preserved ancient sites in the world.

The extensive ruins, located in present-day Libya, is one of the few major archaeological ruins in the world where photographers and tripods are welcome. Unfortunately, the grounds don't open early or stay open late. However, in the winter when rains come, rainwater pools are everywhere. These make great reflections for the great Arch of Severus and the columns surrounding the Hadriatic Baths. Don't miss the very well preserved Medusa heads that were photographed with Brigitte Bardot. I did most of my shooting in the morning here, but late day visits should work as well.

Oceanside Amphitheater of Leptis Magna

The amazing Amphitheater, cut from the cliffs above the ocean, is a wonder of the world, but lies apart from the main ruins. Try to arrive at the amphitheater early enough to have some shadows. Morning is best for shooting the huge bowl (it once held 16,000 people) and a very wide angle lens (I used a 12mm) is ideal to capture the entire bowl in one frame. A panoramic image is also a possibility.

Ubari Lake (Umm-al-Maa) reflection

The Sahara Desert – Libya & Algeria

Many people think of the Sahara Desert as nothing more than endless sand dunes, but in fact there is scenic grandeur galore. The scenic highlights of the Libyan Sahara are at least three: The Acacus Mountains, the Murzuq Sand Sea, and the Ubari Lakes. These features are relatively close together in the southwest part of the country. This huge area would hold up to many repeat visits—the combination of sand and sandstone formations is like nothing else in the world. Add countless natural arches and ancient rock art, and the possibilities are indeed endless.

Camping is the best and only way to shoot these areas, as you will want to be close to sites at sunrise and sunset. Fortunately, guides will camp near the finest locations if they realize that photography is important. In the Acacus Mountains, one of the best locations is the 'Big Arch', a huge span surrounded by dunes,

Left: Arches in Hadrianic Baths

Big arch at night, Jebel Acacus

whose sides conveniently face east and west. Another good Acacus locale is the 'Tripod' or 'Mutant' Arch with three sandstone pillars seeming to grow out of the rock wall. The many rock art sites, along with the amazing Awiss area are also great locations in proximity. At the Awiss, rock formations of every shape rise above sandstone parks and thrust out of huge areas of sand. Though these areas change as the sand shifts, an amazing view can be had when heading north out of the Awiss. To achieve this, you will need to climb a dune and look down on the massive sandstone forms below.

Sandstone dunes, Jebel Acacus

The Murzuq Sand Sea, surrounding the Acacus Mountains, is everyone's dream of what the Sahara should be like. Dune areas of fantastic size are easily navigable by the guides and climbing to the top of the huge ridges of sand at sunrise and sunset allows an infinity of dune forms to be seen and photographed. Some of my best images came at the Ubari Lakes, a string of blue pearls strung out below the endless dunes. The favorite there, Umm al-Maa, reflects the desert sky and the surrounding sands. To get the best angle with the dune behind the lake, shooting in spring or autumn is best. Sunrise is always preferred for reflections in the calm blue waters of this "Mother of Waters."

Just across the border, but accessible only from Algeria, is Tassili n'Ajjer National Park and its crown jewel: the Tadrart. A sea of tall red dunes punctuated by sandstone needles, arches, sandstone "castles", and replete with ancient rock art, it is easily accessible from the oasis town of Djanet. Ironically, the most spectacular dunes and formations: Moula Naga, In Zaouaten, and the giant red dunes of Tin Merzouga are just a stone throw away from the Libyan border; so close, yet so far. Fall is the best time to visit; strong winds usually pick up in early December, making photography more difficult.

A guide is necessary for both the Libyan and Algerian Sahara.

Ancient mud-brick kasbah, Aït Benhaddou

Aït Benhaddou – Morocco

This wonderful desert site is one of my favorites. I first became aware of it in the movie Gladiator, and realized immediately that was a real place and not a computer generated image. I couldn't believe such a cool ancient desert town existed and yet it seemed vaguely familiar from movies like Jesus of Nazareth, Jewel of the Nile, and Lawrence of Arabia.

The site can be shot at sunrise and sunset, but it faces generally southeast, so a sunrise from October through February would work best. During the rest of the year, unless you were shooting from the top of the ruins, the scene would be very backlit and difficult to expose well. Further, the heat becomes unbearable.

One great vantage point is from the terrace on top of the nearby restaurant. A lower view, but also effective, is from the end of the shops that lead down to the streambed. The area is full of people during the day, so I suggest spending the night at the hotel on site to be ready for sunrise. Likely, at that time you will be all alone with this great subject, as I was. Interesting shots can be had inside the Kasbah, but the doors are opened long after sunrise and closed before sunset.

Nearby location: From Aït Benhaddou, it's an easy drive to Merzouga, where you can photograph spectacular dunes at the edge of the vast Sahara desert.

Outer walls of the Medina, Marrakesh

Marrakesh – Morocco

Many sixties survivors think of the lilting Crosby, Stills, and Nash song when they hear of this desert city in North Africa. Though remnants of those glory days still survive, I have often thought that the present Marrakesh more resembles Palm Springs or Las Vegas.

Still, some great landscape photographs can be had here if you can break away from photographing the snake charmers and spice merchants. As for time of year, winter and spring with the snowy Atlas Mountains as a backdrop are probably best. For subjects, I like the huge reflecting pool at Menara Gardens, the Koutoubia Minaret, and the red medina walls shot at sunset with a long lens. Clouds building up over the mountains can provide excellent skies all year for shooting these facets of a legendary city. And don't forget the detail shots: striking doorways, colorful corridors with bounced light, and the lines of ancient buildings. The Hotel La Mamounia is on the

Menara Gardens

short list of the legendary hotels of the world, but it's now quasi-impossible to parley your way in to photograph the fabulous interiors, unless of course you are a guest. You'll have a much easier time at the Jardin Majorelle, a photographer's paradise with striking colors and a huge variety of subject matter. And of course, not even the most hard-core landscape photographers will be able to resist snapping a few street scenes at the Place Jemaa el-Fnaa, where smells, sights, and sounds reach a paroxystic high with few equals in the world.

Door in medina walls

Dead Vlei trees & red dune at sunrise

Namib-Naukluft National Park – Namibia

One of the world's great desert parks, Namib-Naukluft is a haven for African wildlife and a favorite of landscape photographers. The world's highest dunes, located in the park, are not the world's most dramatic although they do have a deep red color. The 'vleis'—areas between the dunes that once held water—are especially exciting for photographers. Sossusvlei and Dead Vlei are photographic wonders. After traveling to Sesriem, which offers visitor services, the paved road ends at a car park at K60. To drive the last 5 kilometers, you'll need a four-wheel drive vehicle. Dead Vlei is just over a mile walk beyond (each way). Sunrise is a great time to visit, but sunset will work equally as well. Spending the night in the Sossusvlei/Dead Vlei area is not allowed; you must drive the 130 kilometers in and out of Sesriem every day and be back before the gate closes.

A great photo opportunity presents itself at Dune 45, 45 kilometers from Sesriem. Dune 45, according to some sources, takes the prize as the most photographed dune in the world. That affirmation is open to serious challenge, in my opinion. I photographed it not knowing this claim, simply because it was a beautiful subject. Doorless helicopter flights above the

Left: Sossusvlei dunes aerial

dunes are great, especially at sunset, and there are balloon trips at sunrise. I also spent a few days shooting in the Naukluft area of the park and did not consider it to be exceptional, save for a few geologic marvels.

Nearby locations: All sites listed here are outside Namib-Naukluft. The Kokerboom Forest preserves a small colony of the amazing trees, some of the most photogenic in the world. Kolmanskop Ghost Town, just outside Luderitz, Namibia, is a former German diamond-mining town being overtaken by the desert sand. Tours are given on a regular basis, but not on Sunday.

Melting snow high in the Cederberg Range

Cederberg Wilderness – South Africa

While walking the trails of Cederberg Wilderness, I never saw another hiker. I seemed to have the whole amazing place to myself.

Climbing up to the 'Maltese Cross' formation in the snow is something I will never forget. On another beautiful morning, I hiked the shorter trail to 'Lot's Wife' at sunrise, an amazing structure with five natural arches. One of these was as thin as a small pipe, circling around above me like a natural arbor. This was the highlight for me, although a hike later in the day at the nearby Matjiesrivier Nature Reserve—which led to a cave arch with four windows and a rock art panel—comes close. Wolfberg Arch, featuring some of the reddest rock in the world, would be a wonderful sunrise shot around the time of either equinox.

Right: Arch framing Cederberg Mountains

Cave Arch, Cederberg Mountains

Cederberg is perhaps the closest I have come to the landscapes of southern Utah, and sometimes we sell images of Cederberg in my Moab, Utah gallery. Visitors are certain these images are from nearby locations. Close to the ocean and far from any significant pollution, expect illumination of amazing beauty and clarity at Cederberg.

Richtersveld Transfrontier Park – South Africa & Namibia

One of the world's great desert national park landscapes, this peace park has mountains and 'kloofs' (deep ravines), some of the best wildflower displays in the world, and the grand canyon of Africa: Fish River Canyon. Two incredible tree species that are fantastic photo subjects are also found here: the kokerboom tree and the halfmens tree.

Aloe on Fish River Canyon rim, Namibia

Moonset on Quiver Tree Forest National Preserve, Namibia

Sendlingsdrif has the easiest access and egress to the South African part of the park with limitless hiking and four-wheel drive roads. Some great park chalets in town make a very comfortable base camp, along with the many tent camps inside the wild desert ranges.

One of my goals (this really shows the difference between landscape and wildlife photographers) was to find and shoot the elusive halfmens tree. This unique tree has features that look almost like a human figure from a distance. If you head out of Sendlingsdrif toward the 'Hand of God' rock formation (not a great photo), you will pass by several stands of these trees. They like to grow in little groups, so if you see one there may be more around. I was fortunate to have some rare clouds to use with the beautiful specimens I found, and when I was there in August the trees were also blooming.

North in Namibia, the Fish River Canyon is a spectacular sunrise and sunset location from the main viewpoint. The deep canyon ridges can be set against the botanical beauty of big red aloes and kokerboom trees growing on the rim. The viewpoint is on the east rim, but the overall scene is so expansive that both early and late-day shots work well. Kokerboom (a.k.a. Quiver trees) are giant aloe trees, which grow in a forest not far from the Fish River Canyon. The living trees make highly photogenic subjects, as do the decaying dead specimens.

Wildflowers in West Coast National Park, South Africa

Namaqualand – South Africa

Where is the world's most prolific wildflower bloom? It could be in South Africa, both in sheer size, and in numbers of species. When you enter a town and flowers cover literally every inch of earth in the village and its surrounding mountains, you feel you've arrived at wildflower planet. The trick is hitting the peak time, the peak year, and the peak place.

Once again, I was extremely lucky, because unpredicted last-minute rains transformed the expected mediocre bloom that year to one of the best. If rainfall totals are good throughout the winter, then your chances for a good flower season are positive. Unfortunately, African weather, like weather everywhere, is becoming more extreme, especially with drought. To further elevate your chances for a good experience, you'll want to give the bloom enough time. I arrived in the second week of August, which is often the beginning of peak bloom in the southern Cape, and stayed for two weeks. Many areas came into bloom during that period. Another strategy for success is to expand your search area. Driving north will lead you to warmer weather and more blooms. Peak can extend to mid-September in the northern region.

Since most of the flower species don't open their petals until mid-morning and close up again in the afternoon, the usual protocol of early and late shooting won't be relevant. Furthermore, most species don't open at all on cloudy days.

Right: Namaqualand wildflowers

The areas that worked best for me included Namaqua National Park, with large areas of pink and orange flowers on the loop road around the Skilpad Wildflower Reserve. Goegap Nature Reserve, offered purple and red blooms. I found extensive flower fields all around the towns of Springbok and Nababeep. To the south, West Coast National Park displayed white and orange African daisies, along both highways 7 and 14.

Remember, you will be there in the springtime and weather can change quickly. A few days after shooting the peak bloom, I was hiking in snow. Many of these national parks have excellent overnight chalets inside the park that are very comfortable and reasonably priced.

Victoria Falls at Danger Point, Zimbabwe

Victoria Falls – Zambia & Zimbabwe

As your airplane crosses the jungle-covered plains you see what appears to be smoke in the distance rising from bush fires. But as you draw closer, you realize it is the rising mists of mighty Victoria Falls.

How things have changed. When I first visited Victoria Falls, the Zimbabwe

Rainbow at Main Falls, Zimbabwe

side was the place to go, and Zambia, on the other side of the river, was to be avoided. Now with troubles in Zimbabwe, many people choose the Zambia side, along with its newer hotels and better infrastructure. The falls in Zambia are basically a mirror image of the falls in Zimbabwe.

The waterfall is oriented southwest to northeast, with most of the falls facing southeast. I was shooting in February, several months before the April peak flow. I think I could have used a little more water in my images, but with as much spray as I was dealing with in February, I fear peak flow (in April) would be a washout for photography and the falls may not even be visible then. My backlit shots are facing in the morning from Zimbabwe while my rainbow shots are accomplished in the afternoon. From Zambia this situation is basically reversed. It's possible to go back and forth between the two countries fairly easily and shoot the best of each. Both sides have lookouts that put you directly in front of the falls.

Make sure to bring something to keep your camera (and yourself) dry. I was initially questioned about my oversized camera equipment by Zimbabwean officials, but they eventually relented and let me enter the falls area.

Rocks on La Digue Island, Seychelles

Anse Source d'Argent – The Seychelles

Anse Source d'Argent on La Digue Island in the Seychelles is the world's most scenic and eminently photographable beach. Located on the southwest corner of La Digue, most visitors to the very small island head here first. For many, the attractions are the gorgeous turquoise water and swaying palms. But the photographer's prize is the amazing sculpted rock formations that line the shore and jut out into the shallow water.

This is not a place where the beach is enhanced by surrounding mountains. Here the focus is on the rocks themselves. Although they cover a small area, the number of compositions seems to be almost unlimited. Shooting here for a week would not become redundant.

Obviously, you won't be alone, but since the beach is on the west side of the island, you may have better luck later in the afternoon when crowds thin out and the light is still good. Full sun would be best with this subject, which is mostly likely to come in the austral winter months. This season will harbinger stiff winds at times, however. Early spring and late fall might be the best time for sun with some clouds and calm waters. Remember that digital cameras are really anathema to salt water, so take care as you may want to stand in the ocean, shooting back to shore. Tripods don't take well to ocean water, either, so I rinse mine with fresh water after exposure.

❖ ❖ ❖

The Treasury, Petra

THE MIDDLE EAST

The Blue Mosque

The Blue Mosque – Istanbul, Turkey

This totally imposing structure sits on the banks of the Black Sea and commands attention from most of Istanbul. My idea for a composition here was to get as high as possible and bring in the water, the opposite shore and mountains to the scene. Many of the hotels on the rising land west of the Mosque have viewing decks and restaurants on their roofs. The hotel where I stayed, the Celal Sultan, has the best possible view of the Hagia Sofia, another famous mosque/museum.

I scouted many hotels for an equally great view of the Blue Mosque, and found the Arcadia Hotel to be the best. Nine floors above the city, its terrace offers a huge panorama of Istanbul. It seemed like a great hotel, and next time I will make it my base of operations. From here, using HDR or a GND filter the mosque is great at sunrise with bright sky behind. This view also works in the morning when clouds appear along the coast, during sunset, and at night. Though the mosque is white, it does take on a blue cast in the morning when backlit and in open shade conditions. Sometimes night-lighting is blue, also.

Pamukkale – Turkey

A strange combination of Grand Canyon's Havasu Canyon and Yellowstone's Mammoth Hot Springs with a ruined Greek city thrown in, Pamukkale is a huge area of white travertine that can be spotted twenty miles away.

Several miles long, the area is heavily controlled and only certain parts may be visited. Once, I started to climb up twenty feet for a better angle on a shot and was whistled at by a guard like a ten-year-old splashing too vigorously in a swimming pool. Tripods are allowed in the mineral spring area but they are not permitted in the ancient ruins of Hierapolis. The pool and white "taffy" area is open 24 hours for great sunrise and sunset shooting.

Water entering the pools is controlled from above, so visiting during spring may be the best time for maximum water and fewer bathers. Winters can be cool and foggy and summer unbearably hot and humid. The whole area is an afternoon to sunset shot for most of the year. Wisely avoid this area on summer weekends.

The nearest hotels of acceptable quality are quite some distance from Pamukkale, but taxis and buses are available. Shooting the blue pools, like the

Blue pools at Pamukkale, Turkey

waters of the Caribbean, is best when the sun is high. A sunset scene, with the sun sinking beyond the western mountains and the travertine pools reflecting the sky, can be a great image.

Cappadocia – Turkey

The Cappadocia region, and in particular the area in Göreme National Park contains Turkey's most beautiful inland scenery, and perhaps the most finely eroded volcanic tuff rocks in the world.

Subjects here include the Fairy Chimneys, balanced rocks that pick up the light beautifully at dawn, in late spring and summer. Three of the chimneys make a good tableau from the top of a small ridge near the parking lot. Since the park area is surrounded by farms and roads, you will have these in the background in most of your shots here. The singular eroded white volcanic tuff formations are on display in many places along the road and on trails. They are at their best at the beginning and end of the day. One of the best vistas is a sunset view on the Uçhisar-Göreme road, along the curves that head up to the hill. Interesting shots of Uçhisar rising castle-like above the sinuous landscape can be

Tufaceous rock formations in Göreme

captured with a long lens from the D302 road in the morning. Outside the park and back towards Ürgüp, another area of balanced rocks is right along side of the road. This again, works best at sunrise or sunset.

Nemrut Dagi – Turkey

Those unfamiliar with this wonder of the world in Eastern Turkey are often amazed when they see my images. At the top of the mountain where the snows feed the Euphrates, an ancient king built a complex of statues that is unlike anything in the world. Contrary to the abstract forms of Easter Island, we know the identity of the deities and people depicted here, which include Greek gods and Alexander the Great.

The many statues were originally seated in a long row about 100 feet high, and bizarrely, the whole scene was created twice,

Zeus & Alexander the Great

Left: The Fairy Chimneys, Göreme

with one row of figures facing the sunrise and another facing the sunset. After more than 2,000 years and countless earthquakes, the great creation is in magnificent shambles. Now the focus of photographic interest is the heads, which

Alexander the Great sculpture, Mt. Nemrut

have survived very well. Zeus in particular, seems larger than the rest and emotes character and godliness. Some of the figures are animals, including visages of lions and raptors. I suggest a visit to both sunrise and sunset sides at the appropriate time. The paved road to the mountaintop allows easy access, and there are good hotels and restaurants just below the park's visitor center. Unlike other Turkish archaeological sites, tripods are allowed at Nemrut Dagi. I suggest you book a tour at Mt. Nemrut. Tours begin in late spring and often continue into the fall. To visit the top of the mountain after a snow is possible according to my guide, and this would add another dimension to this mystical location. You really can't take bad pictures here coming at sunrise and sunset. After shooting overall scenes, I moved in closer and was fascinated by some of the cracked and weathered heads such as Alexander the Great on the sunset side. The spell of Nemrut is pervasive, and you'll find yourself recalling this place long after you come down from this lofty home of gods and heroes. A guide is recommended here.

Nahal David – Israel

Near the Dead Sea in the Judean Desert, one of the Middle East's most beautiful canyons carves its way through the forbidding desert, creating a contrast of lush greenery and waterfalls. At David Spring's source in Ein Gedi Nature Reserve, beautiful waterfalls drop through mosses and ferns and find photogenic channels through the colorful rocks. A hike to Hidden Falls at sunset is the 'piece de resistance'. The canyon narrows and the falls plunge about forty feet into a

Right: Hidden Falls, Ein Gedi Nature Reserve

gorge, while the massive ramparts of the adjacent desert peaks catch the last rays of daylight. Even in the American Southwest, there are few places to shoot a great desert waterfall like this with a canyon rim high above. This hike is great in winter, but would be unimaginably hot in summer. Also, water flow drops significantly during the hot months.

Nearby location: Masada, a storied ruin perched atop a plateau, is a World Heritage Site where the Jews attempted a brave last stand against the Roman Army. The trick to successful photography is being on top with the ruins and the great view of the Dead Sea at sunrise or sunset. Sunset might be easier, as you can take the gondola up and return by foot quickly afterwards. I was able to do the opposite, walking up before sunrise and riding the gondola down later. This is Israel's top tourist site, so expect security checks and lots of people during the middle of the day.

Red Canyon, Eilat Mountains Nature Reserve

Red Canyon – Israel

High in the Eilat Mountains of Israel near the Red Sea and the town of Eilat, one of the world's most colorful canyons beckons your camera. Though the canyon is more purple, pink and yellow than red, the colors change over the course of the day, reaching their peak at sunrise and sunset, when warm light is reflected down into the canyon from above. The walk is short to get there, and compared to most American Southwest canyons, Red Canyon is not very deep.

Nearby location: Timna National Park is north of Eilat along the Great Rift Valley. The area has huge cliffs, pinnacles, and one of the most photogenic double natural arches in the world. It glows like Mesa Arch (near Moab, Utah) at dawn. Rock art dating back to Egyptian times adorns the canyon walls.

Wadi Rum – Jordan

To see Wadi Rum before you visit, watch Lawrence of Arabia. It stars almost as much as Peter O'Toole in that great film. There is much to see and do at Wadi Rum, and it's a place that is worthy of repeat visits. It will remind you of Monument Valley, and is one of the world's great desert scenic areas. I suggest you make Rum Village the base of your explorations, although there are several comfortable Bedouin camps located inside the desert.

Highlights include the Nabataean Temple in close proximity to Rum Village that gets great morning light with a large cliff behind. The Al Ghuroub sunset

Nabataean temple remains, Wadi Rum

site is actually better at sunrise, as it sits to the far northwest of the many buttes and mesas. This viewpoint will work best for side-lighting at dawn in the winter, early spring and late autumn when temperatures are cooler. You will want to hire a guide for your visit to Wadi Rum. Make sure your guide knows that photography is your goal, and that sunrise and sunset are peak times to be out in the Wadi. The guide should also have a four wheel drive vehicle, which is essential for the sandy terrain. Rock art, in the form of petroglyphs, occurs throughout the area.

Winter rains usually subside by mid to late March and in a good year, wildflowers blanket the desert floor in March and April.

Nearby locations: Wadi Mujib is a spectacular slot canyon with a perennial stream ending up in the Dead Sea; it is very reminiscent of the Zion Narrows. You can wade your way up to beautiful waterfalls and pools without canyoneering equipment, but a dry bag is essential for your camera. It is preferable to leave your camera bag with the rangers and take just a point and shoot.

Petra – Jordan

Petra was recently added on the list of places you should visit while it is still accessible, referencing recent civil unrest in the country. However that plays out, if you can visit Petra to photograph, you should. It's high on my list of subjects I'd like to visit again.

There's a strange dynamic in countries like Jordan and Egypt if you are a single traveler. Most people are friendly, but you will probably not escape without-

out some degree of hassle. I remember walking out from my hotel on the beautiful rock formations above the Petra canyons to take a shot, when several men demanded I stop and talk to them. They wanted to tell me that I just couldn't be there without paying them something. When I found a reputable guide, he worked tirelessly to keep people away from me when I was shooting with my 4x5, which always tended to draw a small crowd. Your hotel should be able to fix you up with a good guide

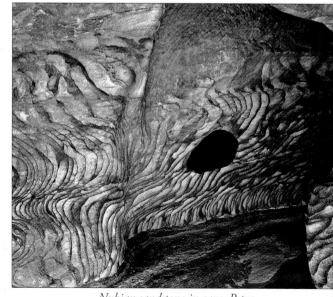

Nubian sandstone in cave, Petra

Left: The Treasury, seen from the Siq

Downtown towers of Doha reflected in rare spring rain, Qatar

who will direct you through the site with little difficulty.

I found three especially enthralling subjects at Petra. The Treasury—accessed through a slot canyon known as the Siq—is the carved facade made famous in The Last Crusade, an Indiana Jones film. It is deep in a canyon itself, and faces southeast, so it is definitely a winter shot in the morning. I used a graduated neutral density filter to block off the sunlit areas of the cliff above the Treasury as the sun slowly made its way into the Wadi (a valley or dry riverbed in Arabic). Some interesting possibilities include climbing up the canyon east of the Treasury to shoot it from above, and using the Siq slot canyon as a framing tool. At other times of the year when the sun is directly overhead and the Treasury is in shade, it picks up fine reflected canyon light, which has strong oranges, reds, and yellows. This effect will be most prominent when the sun is closest to the Treasury without hitting it.

Another favorite subject at Petra is the amazing Nubian sandstone. Its colors, textures, and patterns make great intimate landscapes. Explore the walls around the buildings and notice the rocks as you walk the trails—you'll see many inspiring abstract rock subjects. Third on your list should be Ad-Deir, or the Monastery, which resides outside of the canyons on the mountainside and picks up sunset lighting. It is a somewhat smaller version of the Treasury, but in the same classical style. Though about two miles from the hotel area by trail, it's worthwhile to shoot at sunset here and then head back. It's also worth returning to the site in the evening for the "Petra by Night" sound and light show. It's quite thrilling to walk into the Siq by candlelight and you can shoot high-ISO photographs of the Treasury illuminated by thousands of candles.

The Skyline of Doha – Qatar

I considered the skylines of other Gulf cities with their giant buildings for this book and from a photography standpoint they are indeed spectacular. Although widely still under construction, the other-worldly look of Doha really is in a class by itself. Some may find it garish or outrageous, but to me it looks like the movie visions of George Lucas and other sci-fi films like Metropolis or Blade Runner.

One of my images is a panoramic, a good idea here, and was taken by hand when my tripod didn't arrive with me. I also used some rainwater in the hotel parking lot as a reflecting pool. Water is an unusual element in this desert, where it was 90 degrees in January. The tripod arrived after the water quickly evaporated. So the lesson is: improvise and strike while the iron is hot!

Omanis have a great interest in photography, and they have the means to pursue it seriously. It took nine months to get paid for the workshops I held here. I was told the fee was so small, it just didn't register with anyone.

The Doha desert features a nice natural arch where the sun sets beautifully through the rock window, probably all year long.

Temperatures are mild in winter, but very high with humidity in summer.

Rub' al Khali – Oman

Rub' al Khali (a.k.a. The Empty Quarter) covers parts of several countries. Still not fully explored, it is pure desert, with some of the most beautiful sand dunes I have ever seen. I merely skirted a small corner of the Empty Quarter, but I saw enough to convince me it was a scenic marvel. It also has a strangely calm and

Dunes in the Empty Quarter, Sultanate of Oman

other-worldly quality about it. There are no sounds, no lights, and after leaving the fringes, no signs of vehicles or tracks of any kind. The easiest access is from Oman, where you can visit a small corner of the Empty Quarter as I did.

Geodes on playa floor in the Empty Quarter

Alternately, you can sign on with a tour in Muscat, which is a four-wheel-drive convoy crossing, taking a week or more.

A tour guide is required, but a permit is not and tripods are allowed. Plan for mild winters and very hot summers. No services are available; I mean really none for hundreds of miles in all directions.

Sunset seen from Jebel Akhdar

Jebel Akhdar – Oman

There are many good vantage points to view the Grand Canyon of Oman. Compared to the American Grand Canyon, its Omani counterpart is almost as deep, but much shorter in length. The canyon is a very accessible photo destination with a good road that goes to the viewpoint of the canyon, atop the Hagar Mountains. Even so, there are people that live down inside the canyon who do not know what century it is and have never heard of the outside world. This adds an interesting dimension to an already fascinating place.

A winter sunset with a red sphere sinking over endless Arabian Peninsula ridges is one of the great desert vistas in the world. By the way, winter is really the only time you'll want to visit this part of the world. A nice lodge sits on top of the mountain, where nights can be quite frosty in winter. Mountain Travel/ Sobek and other companies do guided trips here along with local tour operators.

I have shot everywhere in Oman and no one has ever bothered me for any reason. Nobody has asked for compensation for photography, required a permit or tried to restrict my access in any way. Oman is full of secrets, including a desert version of Machu Picchu. I would divulge its location, but I don't think I can find it myself anymore. A guide is recommended here.

Date palms in Wadi Shab

Wadi Shab – Oman

One of the finest canyons in the Mideast, Wadi Shab is a great walk with high walls, swaying date palms, and pools of florescent green water. Oman seems to have a surprising amount of water, considering its desert climate and ferociously hot summers.

The waters of the Shab are best photographed in full sunlight. This is not a problem, however, because I did not see a single cloud during my two visits to

Left: Green pool in Wadi Shab

the country. And I should point out, that unlike your favorite image-editing software, a polarizing filter can capture the full color of the amazing pools. This is the only filter—along with a GND filter—I still carry with me always while shooting.

The palm trees are great subjects, also. In many ways this is a Southwest Canyon, but with unusual trees. As the sun drops lower in the sky, look for great reflections in the still pools. The water even tumbles under a small natural bridge here.

Nearby locations: Other great nearby photo opportunities in Oman include the Slot Canyon of Wadi Quashah, which lights up with brilliant colors at midday. Often full of water and prone to flash flooding, the best time to hike it is during the warmer months. At that time, some of the interior water evaporates or becomes warm enough to swim through.

Karst Landscape near Yangshuo Guangxi

ASIA

Mehrangarh Fort in Jodhpur

Rajasthan – India

This large area of India is truly a magical kingdom, custom-made for landscape photographers. The light is generally very good here, lacking the horrible polluted skies present over much of the rest of the subcontinent. This is especially true outside the monsoon season.

With such a large area to cover and with such daunting logistics, I suggest joining a photo tour to visit and shoot Rajasthan. It's realistically the only way. I traveled by train for this journey and my tour organizers made sure the train pulled into the station before dawn and resumed travel after sunset. Four sites in the region should not be missed: The Amber Fort, The Palace of the Winds, Mehrangarh Fort,

Lake Pichola, Udaipur

and Udaipur Lake. Sunrise is the best time for the Amber Fort and the amazing Mehrangarh Fort, both huge castles atop mountain perches. The Amber Fort may look familiar from the second Indiana Jones movie. The fort even offers a reflecting lake and bougainvillea for complementing elements in your compositions.

Mehrangarh Fort is easily one of India's most amazing scenes at dawn. A small museum area above the main town and to the east of the monolith provides the best view. Scout it the day before, if possible. After sunrise, climb the ramparts of the fort to photograph the blue houses of the surrounding town.

The Palace of the Winds, with such a great name and history, is perhaps my favorite man-made subject in India. Early afternoon, close to the equinoxes, is the best time for good light on the orange-brown facade. Additionally, shopkeepers across the street will most likely let you climb atop their roofs to shoot, if you offer to pay them. This will give you the best vantage point for your image, and help you get above interfering cars, buses and other troublesome elements.

Hawa Mahal (Palace of the Winds) in Jaipur

Udaipur Lake—home to some of the world's most expensive hotels—is interesting, but my least favorite Rajasthan location. Certainly the island palace is intriguing, but not a great scenic photo. Also, the Thar Desert, which many tours take in, is the one desert in this book I cannot endorse enthusiastically.

Tripods are allowed in most places where you are shooting the castles and forts from a distance. Tripods are not allowed, however, inside the palaces.

The Taj Mahal – India

Tripods have never been allowed at the grounds of the Taj Mahal. To shoot the standard view, get to the site long before opening to get as close to the front of the queue as possible. After opening, make your way quickly to the gardens in front of the Taj if you hope to use one of the many reflecting pools to capture a morning reflection.

Due to the air pollution which is common in the area, the morning light is quite soft, but does contain some color. If you can find a good reflection spot, use high ISO and your stabilization system. No matter how soon you arrive,

Taj Mahal at dawn, Agra

you will have people in the photo. Using the content-aware tool in Photoshop can usually help to remove other visitors, if you so desire.

The first shots, with a sunny day (depending on the time of year), will be blue. But since blue sky is at a premium in this part of India, that can be a good thing. As the morning progresses, the sky will become somewhat orange. Side-lighting will appear in spring and autumn, with the light coming from behind you in summer. During the wet season, all bets are off, however. The Baby Taj is often overlooked but is also a superb subject.

Another way to shoot the Taj is to cross the river behind the main grounds and use the river as a reflecting pond. Boats cross the river on a regular basis, but the area is not safe. Make sure you have a trusted guide with you, and whatever you do, do not come in contact with the river water. During the wet season, the river becomes much bigger and compared to the dry season, does not function as well as a reflecting pond. Sometimes, locals bring camels down to pose in front of the Taj Mahal and let them stand in the river, creating additional reflections.

A reliable guide is recommended if you cross the river.

Taj Mahal seen from the Yamuna River

Ajanta & Ellora Caves – India

When I first saw a photo of the Kailasanatha Temple carved from rock like a cousin of Petra, I was compelled to try to photograph it. The Temple itself has a magical ancient quality that is unmatched in India and it is the high point of two areas fairly close together called the Ajanta and Ellora Caves in the Maharashtra area east of Mumbai. Both places are best negotiated with a guide who can help with the logistics and actually get you into places—even with a tripod—that are not normally open to the public. At Ellora, the gigantic carved temple can be photographed at any time of year. The cliff surrounding the huge complex provides great vantage points down over the site and curves around above the sculpted towers below on three sides: east, north, and west. I was allowed to use my tripod on this rimrock view area and in the temple area outside the caves below. For the very best light, consider a winter visit, when the southwest-facing temple would get great sunset lighting. My guide let me enter and use a tripod and natural light in Cave 10, which is the most beautifully carved cave site at Ellora. This whole area would look quite different during the monsoons; I have seen many images of waterfalls coming off the cliffs at both Ajanta and Ellora, adding a nice touch. Though the big temple at Ajanta is completely outdoors, the rock art and carved caves at Ellora are all inside open caves, with very little natural light. The Ellora caves contain paintings of religious subjects and the daily life of Indians sometimes over 2,000 years ago.

Kailasanathar Temple, Ellora

Carved chamber in Ajanta

I have never seen such sophisticated rock art in the world—sometimes bordering or matching renaissance quality. The lighting is a challenge for photographers, although cameras without flash and tripods are allowed in. Try to visit the caves (there are 30, so allow lots of time) during midday when the most light possible is coming from outdoors. Otherwise, you are stuck with the small light strips strung throughout the cave interiors. I set my camera on the tungsten setting, but my jpegs on screen looked very green. I was pleasantly surprised when the temperature and tint controls in Lightroom removed the green cast and yielded images that looked very close to the ones taken by flash. Using high ISO, IS, and VR and focusing with live view are very helpful too. The murals are a little overwhelming in their quantity and quality, but just as you've had enough, the last caves change to great sculpted interiors. These last chambers were basked in outside light when I visited and looked very colorful.

Cave 10 at Ellora

The Himalayas – Nepal

Situated outside the smog and sprawl of Kathmandu, Nagarkot is a small oasis of tranquility and beauty. The attraction here is the panoramic view of the Langtang Range of the Himalayas, often seen above a sea of clouds, One of the hotels there is called the "Hotel at the End of the World," and Nagarkot is built on a cliff that drops down thousands of feet to the valley below. Most hotels have roof-top viewing areas, and since the hotels are all south of the peaks, winter time is the best season to come for shooting both sunrise and sunset. Lots of photographers appear at this time, but most seem intent on shooting distant Everest. Everest is far to the south and just a tiny hump, as viewed from Nagarkot. The magical panorama of the beautiful peaks close by is lost to these photographers.

The "fish tail" of Machapuchare

Lesson: Always keep your eyes open for new material and don't become blindly obsessed with one pre-determined subject or view.

Unfortunately, bad weather never relented during the five days I spent in Nagarkot, and I was unable to bring back any shots worth showing.

Nagarkot is accessible by taxi and a guide is recommended.

Other great viewpoints of the Himalayas include the region around Pokhara. The area near the airport is one of the best to photograph the Annapurnas from a distance, but to get closer to the mountains you'll have to take a short trek. Pokhara is the beginning and end point for treks into the Annapurna Sanctuary, Machapuchare, and the Kali Gandaki river valley. This is considered by many to be one of the most scenic areas in these magnificent mountains.

A short multi-day trek to Ghorepani Pass and the Poon Hill will get you to the

On the Annapurna trail

best views of Machapuchare and Dhaulagiri. Every village along the way has a number of small guesthouses, so you can travel light. Guides and porters are also available to carry your equipment. Return to Pokhara via Ghandruk to visit Gurung country and get closer to the Annapurna Sanctuary.

Closer to Kathmandu is the Dhulikhel Region, also with splendid panoramic views of the Himalayas.

On the eastern side of the Himalayan range, the most interesting location is Darjeeling. Part of the interest is getting up there through the tea plantations with the old narrow-gauge railway. The town itself has a special mountain atmosphere and is very photogenic, but there are long periods of cloudiness and heavy rain. There is a distant view of Kanchengjunga—the third highest summit in the world—but it seems to be eternally shrouded in clouds.

Mt. Everest, Sagarmatha National Park – Nepal

Though not the most scenic mountain in the world, seeing and shooting Mt. Everest is a thrill for most photographers, including me. It's pretty easy these days to shoot the world-famous peak both from the air and from the ground. Like all high peaks, Everest is shy, hiding behind clouds much of the time.

There are conflicting reports on the best time of year to shoot the mountain, but the wet summer season is probably not one of them. I got my shot in December during the dry season. I have to point out, though, if I'd been on the ground instead of in the air, I would not have even seen the mountain.

Mt. Everest and surrounding peaks

After reading a recommendation in a guidebook, I hoped to photograph Everest while on the Druk Air flight that goes from Paro, in Bhutan, to Kathmandu, Nepal. Druk doesn't seem to like providing assigned seats before check-in, so get to the airport early and ask for a seat on the right side, to the rear of the aircraft. After takeoff, if weather is good, you'll be treated to the most scenic flight in the world. If you shoot with a polarizer and a wide-open aperture to blur the dirty windows, the photos will come out surprisingly well. Also, shooting in the winter assures a good sun angle as the airplane follows the front range of the Himalayas, south of the massif. Since there is really nowhere else for the airplane to go but over the Indian lowlands south of the peaks, the flight path should be the same for every trip.

For a ground shot, numerous tour companies offer trips to the Everest base camp—at least that's how they refer to it—driving in from Tibet.

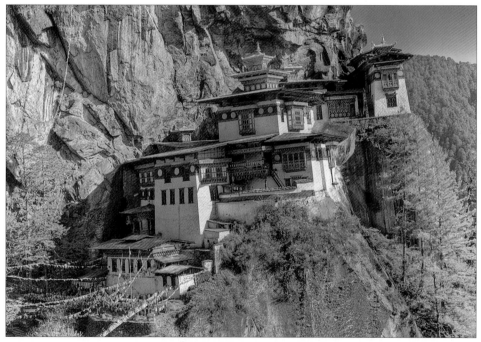

The Tiger's Nest Monastery in Paro Valley

The Tiger's Nest – Bhutan

Except for some of the ancient ruins of the American Southwest, few man-made structures in the world are built as precariously as the Tiger's Nest Monastery in the Himalayan foothills of Bhutan.

Reaching viewpoints requires a strenuous, high-altitude walk up the mountainside to cliffs on the sunset side of the site. A late sunset shot is hardly possible here, as the Tiger's Nest is surrounded on all sides by mountains and cliffs. The viewpoints all face east, so a morning shot here with sun would be backlit unless clouds were present. Alternately, you can shoot in summertime when the cliff would keep the mountain in shade early in the day.

I visited in the winter dry season when I had clear days and a sun angle that cast side-lighting on the subject. Using a wide angle lens at that time of year, composing to include some of the surrounding mountains and the imposing cliff where the Nest resides, works well. During the wet season, this area gets lots of rain, and the surrounding area is essentially a rain forest for part of the year. My guides told me that at that time, fog was a common occurrence. This would add a great deal of mood and mystery to Takstang (the local name of the monastery).

A guide is required here.

Nearby location: The Punakha Dzong, also known as the Palace of Great Happiness. At the confluence of two rivers with blue glacial waters and backed by snowy peaks, the Dzong is very large and beautiful in the unique style of Bhutanese architecture.

Shwedagon Pagoda in Yangon

Shwedagon Pagoda – Myanmar

There are temples, and then there are temples. Nothing really surpasses, in terms of sheer size and complexity, the Shwedagon Pagoda in Yangon (also known as Rangoon).

Like the experience of visiting Myanmar itself, it is somewhat otherworldly.

There's so much color, form, and grandeur, that you could easily spend weeks there.

Like most Asian locales, photography is allowed and welcomed, as are tripods. The Schwedagon Pagoda can be seen at night from many nearby sites in the city. This sets the stage for a great artificial light/natural twilight image. Technical note: Match the light value of the Pagoda's artificial lights with the natural post-sunset light. Unfortunately, I've never photographed there with clouds, which would be a great addition, I'm certain. For your reference, the temple is open until just after sunset, but opens post-sunrise in the morning.

Nearby location: The Royal Boat at Kandawgyi Lake, covered in gold-leaf and resembling a huge temple itself. The lake provides a wonderful reflection of the boat at sunset.

The Golden Rock – Myanmar

I first saw an image of Golden Rock in Myanmar at the airport in Seoul, Korea and became completely captivated by it. Although getting to the Rock is a bit of a journey, there is really nothing like it anywhere else. The Rock is an amazing natural formation: a huge balanced rock on the edge of a mountaintop. Covered in gold leaf, the perilously perched, many thousand ton ball glows magically at sunrise and sunset. Clouds and fog frequently form in and above the nearly pristine forests below.

Golden Rock is a Buddhist pilgrimage site, drawing large numbers of people. This can make photography difficult. They are definitely fewer people at dawn,

The Golden Rock

and the fog is more likely to appear then. So photograph the sunset, but please don't miss the sunrise.

A nice lodge is a short distance away from Golden Rock, but reaching the top of the mountain is not a cake-walk. Large trucks that hold about thirty people make a sometimes hair-raising journey from the base camp up the switchbacks, to the peak. The trucks have hard bench seats and no seatbelts and foreigners are only allowed to go half-way because the last part is so dangerous. Only the Burmese are allowed to stay on the truck. Fortunately, the rest of the way up the mountain is a fairly easy walk, though it would be torridly hot in summer.

Temples at sunrise, Bagan

Bagan – Myanmar

Bagan is a unique archaeological site, scenic wonder and photographic opportunity. When I visited in the month of December, the skies at Bagan were the bluest and cleanest I've seen in eastern Asia. The ancient capital of Burma has so many photographic possibilities with good light that the number of great images to be made here is endless.

Temples at sunset

Since the Bagan Plain is so flat, any way to gain some height with your camera allows you to view and shoot some of the thousands of temples much more effectively. Prior to the early nineties, a large number of temples were open to the public as viewpoints for sunrise and sunset. This may change in the future, but for now, there are only a few, and most of the sunset action is at the Shwesandaw 'stupa'. Get there early to stake out a spot, as buses begin arriving, disgorging hundreds of people while sunset approaches. The southwest corner of the stupa is probably best, and I think the same spot would be just as good at dawn with far fewer visitors.

Another must-do is a sunrise balloon ride. Balloons lift off daily, weather permitting, from September to March. Since each flight is different, I suggest taking two. A 24-100mm lens is probably best for the balloon trip. Don't forget to use high ISO, VR, or IS as you start out with the faint morning light. Drop your ISO back to more normal levels as the landscape brightens.

Koh Tao & Koh Nang Islands

Koh Samui – Thailand

Long ago discovered by the modern world, Koh Samui is both a town and a state of mind. Like the Italians, the Thai really know how to live. A huge tourist draw, this series of islands, protected within Angthong Marine National Park, is easily accessible by a large boat.

Beach on Koh Wua Ta Lap Island

Two island scenes, at least, are worth braving the crowds for. Both require a hike to viewpoints in typically stifling heat. Koh Tao and Koh Nang are twin islands, joined by beautiful reefs and beaches. A fairly easy trail that takes about twenty minutes to walk brings you to the Nang Yuan viewpoint. Here, the scene unfolds. I suggest shooting at Nang Yuan at midday and employing a polarizing filter.

The other island, Koh Wua Talap, is even more beautiful and has fewer human intrusions. A very steep route—I hesitate to call it a trail—goes to the top of the highest point around. Take lots of liquids and be very careful. I injured a hamstring en route here. This required pulling myself up Indiana Jones-style, on the roots of giant fig trees. I wouldn't think this would be a good idea if the trail is wet. Gaining the summit is very steep going, but I can tell you that the best view is from the first viewpoint, not the summit. From the first viewpoint, you have the beach and a beautiful grove of palms with the reef just a few hundred feet below. In the distance, four chains of islands complete the tableau. Go to the top if you desire, but from there everything is just too far away for a good composition.

I have been to Thailand four times, and have never been looked at twice by anyone for shooting with cameras large and small, on a tripod at any location. Also, in coming and going frequently with Bangkok as a hub, I have never had any trouble with my camera equipment in customs.

Nearby location: The Big Buddha, which you can see outside your airplane window as you land. It is big and beautiful in dawn light and open from sunrise until sunset.

Phang Nga (James Bond Island) – Thailand

As mentioned elsewhere in this book, I acquire many of my ideas for landscape subjects from movies and television. Hollywood has a much bigger budget for scouting and location work than I do, and I'm a huge movie fan anyway. While the movie theater is emptied and the credits are still rolling, I'm still in my seat to determine the location for the film.

James Bond Island and its attendant seastack are part of a large area of limestone pinnacles rising out of the ocean near Phuket. As far as I can tell, the area

Seastack at James Bond Island, Phang Nga Bay

was not damaged significantly by the recent tsunami that struck so much of the region. The seastack can be best photographed from the nearby island, reachable on boat tours based north of Phuket. Winter mornings are preferable for this shot. The bay itself is a large and magnificent area, and the best shot I've seen of its many peaks is from an airplane, perhaps available at the Phuket airport.

Nearby locations: Several islands are accessible from nearby Krabi, with offshore seastacks that dwarf the small one at James Bond Island. Also, great beaches and beautifully colored water are part of the milieu. Phi Leh Island, the most famous in the area, is a legendary spot where beautiful tropical bays have been cut into the rock walls of the island. A wide angle lens is needed here to depict the entire scene of the coral waters and the surrounding cliffs. Midday light is best for your visit to Phi Leh Island.

Entrance to Angkor Thom

Angkor Wat – Cambodia

Angkor Wat could easily take the crown of the world's greatest ancient city. It's not as old as some European or African ruins, but the sheer size and complexity of all the temples in the surrounding area are worth at least a week or more of photography. Most travelers arrive by air to nearby Siem Reap, which has metastasized from a small village to a small city, offering everything under the sun to visitors. It has become the gateway to what some consider Asia's most popular tourist attraction.

I visited in the year 2000, when the escalated visitation to Angkor had just begun. I hired a driver and a guide who were overjoyed to have my business. Cambodia is one of the world's poorest countries. When I was there, tripods were allowed and photographers could go anywhere. I have recently heard that the un-restored ruins covered with fig roots, which go so far in expressing the mood of the place, are now off-limits to visitors. The main ruins at Angkor, seen from the beautiful

Bayon Temple Reflection

Right: Strangler Figs Overtaking Ruins

front facade, face west for optimum sunset shooting. At certain times of the year, there are reflecting pools at prime places in front of the ruins. Climbing the nearby hill at sunset to the west of the main ruins, and using a long lens, provides a view of the tallest parts of the city rising from the endless jungle. Roaming the corridors of the main ruins when light is good, offers countless opportunities for close-ups and intimate details of the bas-relief and sculpted figures on the walls.

The nearby sister city of Angkor Thom has a magnificent entrance of carved spirit figures. With a 4x5 camera, I was able to get eight inches away from the closest figure and extend focus all the way to the back of the entrance area. You can imitate this digitally, with digital focus-stacking programs. Many of the vine-covered ruins are in this city along with the Bayon Temple, which unlike Angkor, faces east for a sunrise shot. Several miles outside of town, your driver can take you to Banteay Srei, a smaller temple with wonderfully intricate detail.

Luang Prabang – Laos

The entire town of Luang Prabang, one of Asia's best preserved historic villages, is a World Heritage Site. The ever present Mekong River is part of the

Tree of Life Mosaic, Wat Xieng Thong

Mosaic detail, Wat Xieng Thong

scene, passing flowery groves in spring on its way towards the nearby mountains.

There are many photo opportunities in the city, but two stand out. Wat Xieng Thong and its tree of life mosaic from the 16th century are colorful and inspiring. Other mosaics on the Wat and associated buildings depict outdoor subjects and are blindingly colorful. Soft light is best for these, but early morning light on the east-facing red-orange tree of life is astounding. Wat Xieng Thong is open at all times.

My other favorite spot, the Pak Ou Caves, require a short boat ride down the Mekong River. The caves contain thousands of Buddha figures inside the cave, facing toward the river. I used HDR to capture the poorly-lit cave interior and the bright outdoor river in the same scene. A guide is helpful here because few people speak English, and certain formalities are important. As with most Asian sites, no one cared that I used a tripod extensively. Photography is not considered to be a crime or a sin here.

Unfortunately, all of Southeast Asia seems to be covered in smog from China and the burning of local forests. This happens in the winter and spring and perhaps other times, as well. Dealing with this issue photographically can be a challenge.

I recommend a guide at Luang Prabang.

Limestone pinnacles in Ha Long Bay

Ha Long Bay, Viet Nam

Ha Long Bay is Viet Nam's most photogenic natural wonder. Thousands of limestone pinnacles, big and small, rise out of the shallow green ocean bay. Traveling among the formations is only done by boat. Visitors can choose from "cruises", usually lasting only a day or two, or rent a boat to travel on your own. The third option is to do both, as I chose.

I first visited the Bay in March, and had very little sunlight. During this time of year, a foggy haze travels down from China and can linger for weeks. There was no wind, making reflections good, and the fog sometimes had the surreal effect of making the horizon line disappear, an effect I liked. Spring and summer might be more advantageous to photography, although the Bay is a frequent

target for storms that halt all travel there. Ha Long Bay is a place that deserves repeated visits, and I would like to return during a sunnier period, to try my fortune again.

Nearby location: Surprise Cave, which is usually included with a Ha Long Bay cruise, is beautiful, extremely colorful, and open to photographers with tripods. You'll have plenty of time to walk through the cave and shoot a number of formations including the scalloped ceiling. This must have been ocean-formed and is a feature I have not seen in any other cave. You'll need a wide angle lens to show the ceiling off to its full advantage.

Pura Luhur Uluwatu, high above Bali Strait

Pura Ulun Danu Bratan Temple, Bali – Indonesia

This lovely temple on Lake Bratan, reflected in the water with a little fog and the blue mountains behind, is the best shot on Bali. Getting to the spot will require that your guide collects you before dawn. You must have a calm morning for the reflection, with strong sunlight. The summer months are less than ideal here, as the sun's position will create an undesirable backlit situation at the small lakeside area where you will be shooting. A GND filter or shooting in HDR will also be helpful for this subject. A guide is required.

Nearby locations: The other Bali temples and rice terraces are probably the most exciting landscape photography subjects on Bali. Some of the amazing temples like Pura Taman Ayun, are very black, and will benefit from HDR—and should be much easier shot digitally than the film I used. Though very small, the Pura Luhur Uluwatu Temple, high above the ocean, is a great location at sunset.

Pura Ulun Danu Bratan Temple

The cliffs and the ocean facing west enjoy a great sunset glow there, although the angle of the sun for this shot will be best outside the winter months. In July and August, water will fill the rice terraces in Bali, making them the most photogenic. In September, the terraces are a lush green. Your guide can take you to a number of good locations to shoot the terraces, and a long lens is often desired.

The Monkey Forest, in Ubud, may sound like a tourist trap, but it is a wonderful location in a deep tropical forest and you won't resist observing and photographing the antics of the hundreds of monkeys that populate the forest. Furthermore, the entrance to the forest is located smack in the center of Ubud.

As we are on the subject of monkeys, you'll not want to miss a 'ketjak' dance. Dances are held all over the island for a small fee and photography is welcome.

Mount Batur, one of Bali's active volcanoes, and its namesake crater lake are only a short drive from Ubud and can yield nice pictures at sunrise or sunset.

Bromo Volcano & East Java – Indonesia

The Bromo is easily one of the most spectacular volcanoes in the world—seen at close range from the top of the caldera, as well as from a distance. It used to be a long and eventful drive by truck all the way from Surabaya, but you can now stay in comfort in the nearby village of Cemorolawang, from where you can reach the volcano on foot or by jeep. The jeep tour is the most practical to catch sunrise, but for hardy souls willing to wake up at 3AM, I recommend the under 1-hour walk across the "Sea of Sand", an utterly moonlike experience culminating in a short ascent (on steps) to the inner caldera. The view into the crater from the caldera is spectacular. Bromo is an active volcano and has a history of violent

Right: Mount Bromo

Borobudur stupas

eruptions. In recent years it has forced evacuations and cancelled flights, but most of the time it only releases a plume of gases that makes it very photogenic. Such is the case of other very active East Java volcanoes like Merapi, which created massive havoc and deaths in its powerful 2010 eruption.

Nearby locations: Java has a rich history spanning at least two millenaries. It is the main area outside of India where Hindu and Buddhist cultures have taken such a hold. Dieng Plateau, northwest of Yogyakarta, has a number of Hindu temples set on a volcanic plain, dating back to the 8th century. On the outskirts of Yogya—as it is known to the locals—Prambanan and its adjacent towers is the largest Hindu temple in southeast Asia and extremely photogenic. A bit farther west is Borobudur, the largest Buddhist temple in the world, with its characteristic 'stupas' and beautifully carved statues of the Buddha. Yogya itself is a fascinating place; the center of the sophisticated Javanese culture, its royal palace, or Kraton, offers great photography.

The Chocolate Hills – The Philippines

I saw an image once of the Chocolate Hills in a Filipino restaurant in Salt Lake City and was immediately impressed by the unusual landscape. Almost 2,000 of the symmetrical, dome-like hills occupy a large area on the island of Bohol.

The standard viewpoint is a high vantage called Sagbayan Peak which allows you to photograph with good subject side-lighting at sunrise in winter. In summer, your view from the Peak might show too much backlighting to be optimal at sunrise and sunset. A normal or telephoto lens would work well here, as there is no foreground material to create depth. In the summer wet season, the hills are very green and commonly foggy in the morning. During the dry season, they can take on a very red appearance. Another viewpoint which I didn't think was quite as good, but worth a look, is called Carmen and not far from Sagbayan.

Uplifted and eroded Coral deposits, Chocolate Hills

Limestone pinnacle on Thing Beach, Bacuit Bay

El Nido – The Philippines

I often think of places I visit overseas as combinations of places I've already been to or know well. For example, I think of Arnhem Land in Australia as 'The Needles' in Canyonlands National Park combined with the Everglades, or Sweden as Minnesota combined with New England.

El Nido to me is the Great Barrier Reef combined with Monument Valley. Everywhere you look, Monument Valley-esque buttes rise above the tropical waters. A water taxi dropped me on an island in the middle of all this, and I stayed at a beautiful but inexpensive resort. They gave me my own motorboat to tour the bays and beaches nearby. One of the beaches, called Helicopter Island, was blood red,

Pink beach on Helicopter Island, Bacuit Bay

surpassing even the pink beaches of the Bahamas. At Big Lagoon, a trail leads to a ridge with magnificent views of the jungle-covered peaks and mesas that emerge from the ocean. At a small sea cave, we entered into a large pool surrounded by monolithic rock walls. I photographed a strange "knobby" starfish with my 4x5 on the beaches there—a small vignette in a big place.

Hong Kong seen from the Peak

The Peak – Hong Kong, China

The view of Hong Kong from The Peak is one of the best city views in the world. Scores of buildings, a huge harbor and mountains in the distance all combine to produce a powerful scene.

It's easy to get a taxi to the location, though good weather and visibility are sometimes a problem. I was amazed, however, at the clarity of the air I found here after fighting the horrible air of mainland China for several weeks. I believe I can thank the fresh breezes coming in from the ocean for the clarity and blue skies. Also, I had magnificent clouds and great sunset light (the Peak being an afternoon and evening location). There is plenty of room at the Peak viewpoint, but buses do arrive every few minutes with hordes of visitors. Hang on to your tripod.

Nearby location: The view of the city skyline from across Victoria Harbor at dawn. You'll have few competitors for a tripod slot here. Clouds hanging around the nearby mountains often light up colorfully above the skyscrapers.

Wildflower field & Karst landscape near Yangshuo Guangxi

Guilin & Yangshuo – China

Few places on Earth are such a showcase for limestone as the area around Guilin and Yangshuo, China. Though Guilin is more often mentioned when the iconic karst landscape is discussed in travel circles, the area between Guilin and Yangshuo, and Yangshuo itself, is really more in the thick of the beauty.

Limestone arch

When I first visited the area, I quickly changed my working base to Yangshuo. The boat trip from Guilin to Yangshou on the Li River is a great idea. This is especially true if it has been raining, because waterfalls are everywhere. Hiring a guide in Guilin or Yangshuo to take you to nearby small towns surrounded by the amazing pinnacles is really the best way to visit the out-of-the-way spots. Make sure your guide in Yangshuo takes you on a hike to Moon Hill, where a huge natural arch frames distant limestone peaks.

A guide is recommended.

The Yuanyang Rice Terraces – China

In size, variety, and surrounding beauty, the Yuanyang Rice Terraces are unsurpassed. Furthermore, recent road upgrades have made visiting them much easier. Now only a few hours from Kunming, no photographer visiting China should miss this location, and no other rice terraces that I've seen or visited, measure up to this one.

At one sunrise site, you can shoot from the world's only 'photographer's stadium', where part of the hill has been filled with tiers allowing hundreds of photographers to set up and shoot over each other. If that sounds a little outrageous, there were probably only about thirty people there when I visited. And during my week of shooting the terraces—they certainly deserve that long—I did not see one other non-Asian. There are so many fields I never felt crowded, and conditions changed so much with fog, clouds, rain and sun, that everything was in constant flux. Somehow, just by luck, I was visiting during the time when the

Aerial view of Yuanyang rice terraces

terraces were filled with water. I saw pictures of the terraces in fall that looked great, but I don't think any other time of year would surpass the 'wet-terrace' season. In the year I visited, this occurred mid-March.

Guides are really essential here, because the roads are so complex and circuitous. Literally, I never knew where we were. All the guides have worked with photographers and know where to be at the most advantageous times. Except when shooting with wide angle lenses to include the surrounding mountains as background, longer glass seemed to be the most effective tool.

You'll be amazed at how the water color changes through the course of the day, so be ready. At dawn and sunset the terraces are sometimes golden or pink. At predawn and after sunset they're a deep blue, while in the middle of the day the greens of the terraces come to fore as the water turns gray.

I can honestly say that the Yuan Yang Rice Terraces are one of the most artistically satisfying locations I have ever photographed.

Wulingyuan National Park – China

This park is likely the most amazing place in the book you've never heard of. You have seen it though, since it was one of the major inspirations for the "Floating Mountains" in the movie Avatar. Famous in Asia and a favorite of Koreans, it pulls huge numbers of visitors in the summer months. By contrast, when I visited in March, I was the only person in the hotel.

This is a large park with many facets, and lighting and weather changes have a sizable impact. Like Huangshan, its sister park, fog is very effective in causing the rock formations in Wulingyuan to appear like Asian art. And rock formations abound: over 3,000 pinnacles soar as high as one half-mile above the valley floor. Access to the viewpoints on the top of the plateau is mainly by cable car and a crazy elevator. You can expect the typically humorous Asian names for

the viewpoints, but the "Front Garden" is an especially scenic place within the Zhangjiajie portion of the park.

Shooting the pinnacles works well with both back-lighting and side-lighting. Your angle from the viewpoints to the Front Garden is from the southeast.

The other main viewpoint area is the Emperor Mountain district, directly northeast and a long drive around to its entrance. The viewpoint here is stunning, and it is possible to spend the

Rock pinnacles in Zhangjiajie National Forest

Left: Huangshan pines & peaks

night at the top to shoot both sunset and sunrise. One canyon on this side of the park, "Fairies Presenting Bouquets", has hundreds of colorful pinnacles. The thin, towering Imperial Pen Peak is also a highlight.

Your photography here would clearly benefit from repeated visits. There are lush greens in spring, leaf color in the fall and snow in winter. Also, the lower levels of the park have great natural arches, reflecting pools and rice terraces. Access to the interior of the park is by cable car from the park entrance, unless you're spending the night on top, shooting time is tied to cable car schedules.

Although this is far from a Chinese backwater, few people speak English. Don't even attempt to visit this park without an English-speaking guide. Also, though the hotels are comfortable, there is nothing resembling Western food. If you do not appreciate authentic Chinese food, you may be in trouble. Avoid the trailside food kiosks. I got deathly ill from eating from them.

Huangshan Mountains in late afernoon

The Huangshan Mountains – China

The Huangshan Mountains of China are the place to go for landscapes that have the look and feel of the Orient. You've very likely seen this place before in Chinese art, as it's been a favorite subject for centuries. My endeavors there produced photographs that are almost indistinguishable from paintings.

Fog-shrouded peaks, Huangshan Mountains

The location of the range is favorable for an almost constant influx of fog, shrouding the trees and granite peaks with a constantly changing aura of mystery. The viewpoints have charming names that border on humorous, but it's hard to recommend one from the other, as the scene is almost always changing. An elevator system takes visitors to the top at one point in the range, and you can walk to all the vistas from there. Seasonal changes at Huangshan are great opportunities, with good snows in the winter and excellent fall color. Also, the Huangshan pine is an extremely photogenic species that adds interest to big scenics. They are excellent individual subjects, as well.

The best idea is to spend the night. Stay at the best hotel you can up on top, unless you want really traditional Chinese food, which I don't care for.

A guide is recommended here.

Xian's Terracotta Army – China

This singular archaeological site blurs the line between indoor and outdoor subjects. I include it because even though the warriors and horses are covered to protect them from weather, it is easy to shoot them with the natural light entering the main viewing area.

When I visited many years ago, I was charged $100 for my tripod and told

Terracotta warriors & horses

I could shoot three shots. I stretched it out to five or six. I understand the rules change constantly here, so I can't guarantee you'll be allowed a tripod by the time you read this. On the positive side, I read a 2009 blog by a Chinese photographer recommending the use of a tripod, without any mention of a fee. There should be an acceptable amount of light sans tripod, however, if you employ a higher ISO plus image stabilization (or vibration reduction) to get a good shot. The sunlight is diffused here, so photographing at midday would provide the optimum illumination. Panoramic images are also a good choice, as the warriors are stretched out on both sides of the viewing area.

The Great Wall – China

The Mutianyu portion of the Great Wall of China is one of the most accessible areas to visit along this world-famous monument. Although the number of

Right: the Great Wall at Mutianyu

tourists has increased considerably since I first visited many years ago, it can still seem deserted at certain times of the day and year. When you compare the Mutianyu portion to the Badaling area of the Wall, closer to Beijing, this is especially true. With a lot of lush greenery in summer and a very long view of the Great Wall, Mutianyu is the clear winner in my book. Mutianyu requires a two hour drive from Beijing.

Seasonal changes can be very instrumental here. One of the best landscape photography techniques is to visit any great area like The Great Wall, and try to predict what can happen with spring greens, autumn colors and winter snows. You can then plan a return to take advantage of the seasonal changes. This section of the Wall would shine with all these varying attributes.

Prepare for a lot of uphill walking at the Great Wall. Follow the steps up to the highest areas to the left of the parking lot to record great light on clear days. Your best chance is after a storm comes through and cleans the air. Using a driver and guide here can be helpful in getting you in place and allowing you to stay to take advantage of sunset light.

The use of a guide is recommended here.

The Floating Torii of Miyajima – Japan

Lovely Miyajima Island, just off the coast of Japan near Hiroshima, harbors one of Japan's most important and striking shrines: the Floating Torii. Surrounded by mountains, the Floating Torii is situated just offshore so that the tide water leaves it stranded at times and partially submerged at others. Its overall effect is one of timeless peace.

I spent several days capturing this image, waiting for the tide to be just right to take a twilight shot. Here, the Torii is lit artificially, and the ocean is calm and shallow enough to allow a reflection. I had planned my trip to arrive during cherry blossom season, so I had many opportunities to photograph the nearby temple

Left & anbove: The Floating Torii, Miyajima Island

with the trees. One day, I climbed to the top of the mountain, where monkeys tried to steal lenses out of my backpack.

In Japan, every time I set up a shot with my 4x5 camera in public, I drew a crowd. I sensed a feeling of veneration from the people who watched me. I suppose since photography is so respected in Japan, they thought someone with such a big, unusual camera must be a master. I also took a liking to sake while I was there, but during the rainy days, with little other than sumo wrestling on television, I got very bored. Thank heavens for the entertainment we can now carry with us on computers and tablets. At last, though, the time to shoot came with favorable weather and cooperating tides. I used the old technique of matching the light beamed on the shrine with the twilight behind. When my light meter said they were equal, I captured my image.

Mt. Fuji reflection

Mt. Fuji – Japan

The Japanese have done a good job of photographing Mount Fuji. Photo books abound with great images of the iconic mountain showing spring blossoms, lightning storms, snowy cities at its base, and great reflections.

I was able to get a little different image of the mountain by waiting several days and visiting in the spring when the mountain was covered with a winter's worth of snow. I stayed at a bed and breakfast at the base of Fuji. Getting there was not easy on my own, as I worked my way through the Tokyo train system out to the mountain. Fortunately, my host came to the train station to get me and all was well. Over the next few days, eschewing taxis that were not in my price range, I walked all over the area looking for something to use with the mountain. At last, I came upon a small lake which reflected the peak at dawn. After several days waiting through clouds and fog there, I succeeded in getting the shot I had envisioned.

Shooting Fuji is not easy. Surrounded by a city, and obscured by weather from the nearby ocean, it might take a long time to capture a quality image. The best shots I saw were in winter, with beautiful snow on the forest at its base, in spring with a sprig of blossoms in the foreground, and in autumn with a touch of fall color. As for my shot, the editor of the most famous photography magazine in the world ordered a print of it from me. He said looking at the image gave him an inner calm, ironically the opposite feeling I got from my time in Tokyo.

Kamchatka Peninsula – Russian Federation

Kamchatka is the only place in this book I visited but did not photograph. After a long journey, I was prepared to fly, via helicopter, to the Valley of Geysers and over the many volcanoes. Unfortunately, a strange infection felled me and I was quickly taken back to Vladivostok.

The main attraction here for photographers is a huge wild area and the largest concentration of active volcanoes in the world. A dizzying number of parks, reserves, and biological preserves cover the area. I learned a great deal about the area during my trip preparation process. First, it is a difficult and expensive place to get to, and the season for travel overland is very short: from mid-July to the end of August. Difficulties during this time include hordes of mosquitoes, fierce winds, and active grizzly bears. Some roads are open to allow access to hikes and the interior of the peninsula.

One place that should be a major goal for any photographer is a mini Yellowstone, called the Valley of the Geysers. It is accessible by one-day helicopter trips and long hikes. The colors and geothermal activity of the area are world-class and eminently photogenic. Other classic scenes include aerial views of the amazing cobalt-blue volcanic crater lakes, some consisting of sulfuric acid instead of water. Kamchatka is so big that travel by helicopter to some of the best sites can be very costly. Local tour operators offer helicopter ski trips in the winter, and it may be possible to hitch a ride on one of these to shoot photos more economically.

Permits are required, not for photography per se, but for visitation to the area.

Inside Mini Palms Gorge, Purnululu National Park

AUSTRALIA

Echo Point, Blue Mountains National Park

The Blue Mountains – New South Wales

This large collection of parks, just outside of Sydney, is a maze of wooded canyons cut into the Dividing Ranges. When rains come, waterfalls are everywhere. Slot canyons, requiring canyoneering skills, are tucked back in many of the defiles. The Ranges, actually low mountains, protect the coast of Australia form the formidable desert that lies beyond.

Near Katoomba, two of the best

Fitzroy Falls, Morton National Park

photographic attractions are the Three Sisters rock formations and Wentworth Falls. The Three Sisters canyon is sometimes filled with fog but this makes a great dawn subject in summer, with the pinnacles appearing to rise up above the fog sea. Other mesas in the distance also rear up amidst the fog.

Wentworth Falls is heavily dependent on rain and is probably best photographed in winter. I was there during a day-long summer downpour that barely produced a flow at Wentworth.

Fitzroy Falls in Morton National Park, further south, however, seems to always be flowing well and gushes over the rim of a beautiful green canyon. It can be shot from across the canyon by road, or by a short walk to where it plunges off the cliffs.

Lichen on Shore Rocks at the Gardens, Bay of Fires

The Tasmanian Coast – Tasmania

The Coast of Tasmania is one of the most scenic locations I have encountered, with amazing geologic wonders, and some of the cleanest air in the world. A lot of great Australian nature and landscape photographers live in Hobart and surrounding areas, and there's a reason why.

Most of the great coastal scenery is clustered around the southeast coast of the

island in Tasman National Park. The most accessible photo opportunity is the Tessellated Pavement, an puzzlingly beautiful area of square Euclidean patterns eroded out of the shore rocks. Try to shoot the Pavement at dawn and on a morning with low tide. The site is right next to the Arthur Highway, and easy to scout beforehand. If you have some great morning clouds and use HDR or a GND filter, you'll have some excellent results with reflections in the rectangular pools. Shoot in the morning toward the south or north with the rock patterns as a foreground, which also works well.

Tessellated Pavement in dawn light

A few miles away on the Tasman Peninsula, a short road and a trail take you to Tasmans Arch, Australia's best sea arch. Walking a little further on the Peninsula to the south will lead to Waterfall Bay. To be here after a big rain is a photographic treat, as dozens of waterfalls crash down to the sea, making an incredible scene. The end of the peninsula, called Cape Huay, is an area best explored by boat on a calm day. It is also reachable on foot.

Several world-class seastacks, including the Totem Pole—a thin spire—can be seen and photographed at the end of the Peninsula. With a Zodiac boat, it might be possible to land, or otherwise, get a good shot of the Totem Pole from the ocean. Come in summer at midday, as the thin spire formation is surrounded by rock walls. Cape Raoul, another "lands end" area of the Tasman Peninsula, is a long walk, but well worth visiting and photographing. Take plenty of water in summer, and go all the way out to a view of the final cliff wall, one of the most magnificent

Vertical cliffs at Cape Raoul

Left: Tessellated pavement in dawn light

seacliffs in the world. One length of the wall faces southwest, making an excellent late day shot in summer.

Farther north in Tasmania, in Freycinet National park, a great objective is Wineglass Bay. The gorgeous blue waters of the bay can be seen from above on the trail, and it makes an excellent aerial subject. In far northeast Tasmania, at a place called the Gardens along the Bay of Fires, look for shore rocks with some of the world's most beautiful lichen. Since most of the colorful stuff seems to grow on the west side of the shore rocks, away from the ocean, sunset is the preferred time here. The rocks also look great under overcast conditions, and when the lichen is wet.

The Twelve Apostles, Port Cambell National Park

The Twelve Apostles, Port Campbell National Park – Victoria

The Twelve Apostles—there are actually eight, by the way—are a collection of seastacks on the Victoria Coast. Unfortunately, the closest stack to the parking area, and the most beautiful, fell down in 2005. The special nature of the area was diminished somewhat by this event, but it still has much to offer. The stacks are especially appealing backlit, with a setting sun. Be advised however, this only happens in winter months when the sun is in the north. Visitors are not allowed on the beach below, at any time.

Nearby locations: Port Campbell National Park has more seastacks and beautiful seascapes. Otway National Park, on the route back to Melbourne, is famous for its forests and many waterfalls. The falls are most vigorous during the winter rainy season, naturally.

Other great seastacks around the globe include Dunbristy, just off the coast at Downpatrick Head in County Mayo, Ireland. Dunbristy can be reached by a short walk from the car park. Two of the world's largest seastacks are off Duncansby Head in Northern Scotland. For the best light at Duncansby, a pre-dawn hike on a clear summer day is highly recommended.

The Pinnacles Desert, Nambung Nat'l Park – Western Australia

If I were rating the photographic locales featured in this book, Nambung National Park would rank near the top. Combine a fantastic subject with ever-changing and often great light – that's Nambung.

My signature image from Nambung looks like it was taken on Mars. Probably the first thing you'll notice after you get over the acres of amazing stone spires is

Sunset in the Pinnaacles Desert

the orange sand. It looks artificially colored in photos, but it really is that orange. I have spent weeks at Nambung, and never thought I was repeating myself. Besides the geology, its proximity to the Indian Ocean provides an ever-changing backdrop for the amazing needles. My best advice is to just go out exploring during the golden hours of early and late light. You'll find shots everywhere. Fog is common, adding another layer of mystery to this wondrous place.

Visiting Nambung is very easy. Camping is not allowed in the park, so book a hotel in nearby Cervantes. Also try some of the local lobster. The only danger at Nambung is the large number of wild animals that appear on the road during the pre-dawn and post-sunset hours, just when you will be driving. Take extreme care in traveling by car and slow down to a crawl for the entire trip out and back.

The Pinnacles Desert is accessible by car and most services are available.

Morning clouds in the Pinnacles Desert

Red walls inside Weano Gorge

Karijini National Park – Western Australia

Karijini is a great desert park, and one of Australia's gems. However, it is quite remote and has several gorges that are dangerous and potentially deadly. My daughter sustained a serious injury in Hancock Gorge and actually had to be evacuated. In spite of our bad experience, there's a lot of great photography here, and it's a place I would return to without question.

Formerly called the Hammersly Ranges, visiting Karijini is probably best after the rainy season is over and roads are passable. As you might imagine, however, there are trade-offs with each season. Right after the wet season, the roads might still be difficult to navigate, but the waterfalls you can see from viewpoints will be very beautiful with lots of flow. At the same time, some of the slot canyons containing water may be impassable until the level drops later in the season. At that time, the roads should be good and the narrow canyons more easily passable, but the big waterfalls may have shrunken to mere dribbles. This was the case when I visited in August.

Starting with the easiest photo opportunities, the view of Knox Gorge near the carpark is a great sunset shot, especially with HDR. Another short walk takes you to a view of Joffre Falls, a beautiful stairstep cascade. A trail takes you to the top of the falls, which was not running well when I visited there. An even more accessible subject is Fortesque Falls, which had more water than Joffre, but was not on the same large scale. Located near the campground, Fortesque was easy to walk to, however.

Oxers Lookout view, Karijini National Park

Turning to the more difficult hikes, Hancock Gorge is definitely the photographic highlight of the park. It's possible to walk down a short distance into Hancock Gorge until you are blocked by a large pool. The light at the end of the easy trail at noon is great with HDR. The green pool blocking your advance becomes lit and provides beautiful slot canyon lighting for the "room" it occupies. From here on, I suggest hiring a guide or joining a tour to get you through the many obstacles encountered in the remainder of the gorge. For me, photography became secondary to rappelling, swimming and climbing, so I didn't get that many shots in the lower gorge. Of course, I was using a 4x5 camera, and the new waterproof digital cameras would be much better suited for shooting in the rest of these amazing canyons.

The Kimberly – Western Australia

A region of Western Australia, the Kimberly is the wildest and most impressive corner of the Australian continent. Nature is in control here. If you saw the movie Australia, you saw some hints of this part of the Outback. This is a huge area.

From Broome with its endless beach, drive up the peninsula to Cape Leveque and shoot the world's best red rock formations next to a wild beach.

Right: Hidden Falls, El Questro Wilderness Park

Concentric circle pictographs, El Questro Wilderness Park

Be advised, though, you should book lodging far in advance to stay here. Perhaps the best, but most expensive way to explore the Kimberly is by boat. This is the only way to see King George Falls, two massive waterfalls gushing over red rock cliffs into the ocean. Most tours offer helicopter trips to Mitchell Falls National Park, another amazing falls. Land tours to Mitchell and helicopter tours from the mainland also may allow a night camping near the falls to shoot it in sunset and sunrise light.

With both land and water tours, ancient rock art sites are visited, some only accessible by boat. The Kimberly is home to a number of great canyons like Tunnel Creek, Windjana Gorge, Geike Gorge, and perhaps one of the world's most beautiful waterfalls: Emma Gorge at El Questro Wilderness Ranch. Though a huge cyclone flood hit the gorge several years ago, I'm sure it has returned to its former beauty. The falls are a thin cascade surrounded by the greenest walls imaginable. It is a short walk from the Emma Gorge Hotel and Restaurant. Morning is the best time to visit Emma Gorge. All these falls will be at their highest flow and strongest visibility in the late spring, if the wet season has been truly wet.

For much of the year, the Kimberly is virtually off limits to land travel due to the wet season rains from January to May, and the horrendous heat and humidity.

In May and June, the waterfalls will be at their maximum. Through the winter, expect clear, warm days and cool, sometimes cold nights. This is all speculative, as I have seen amazing waterfalls and bad roads continuing into August after a particularly heavy wet season.

New wonders are still being discovered in the Kimberly. On a helicopter tour of El Questro, I was shown a recently discovered waterfall falling in jumps over rock as red as blood. See also the entry for Purnululu National Park.

Sunset at Cape Leveque

Permits are required for professionals at Mitchell Falls National Park. With careful planning and wilderness skills, this country can be explored on your own, but I recommend a guide or a guided tour.

Purnululu National Park – Western Australia

Part of Baz Luhrmann's magnificent movie, Australia, was filmed in Purnululu (a.k.a. the Bungle Bungles), one of the most scenic national parks on the continent. Of course the huge natural arch and the bottomless gorge in the movie were CGI (computer generated imagery), but the real thing is just as good.

Aerial view of the Bungle Bungles

Moon and arch

Unless you come in by helicopter, the hardest part of visiting the Bungle Bungles is the long drive in. The park is also subject to the wet/dry weather paradigm of north Australia. I think the best time to visit is August, when roads are usually passable, the days are gorgeous and the nights are cool. A great little campground/restaurant in the park is also open at this time of year, offering rest and sustenance after your long hikes through the striped domes of this rock wonderland. Americans will find it similar to Southwestern canyon country, except that instead of cottonwoods and junipers, you'll find palm trees surrounding the desert pools.

Several great walks with photographic opportunities include Cathedral Gorge (good at midday with reflected slot-canyon light), Echidna Chasm, a real slot canyon also good at midday, and Mini-Palms Gorge.

Helicopters are always available for sunrise or sunset aerial shooting—the only true way to view the thousands of rock domes that make up the heart of the park. A few miles away, the chopper will take you over a huge, free-standing natural arch seeming to grow up, right out of the sand. Later, I asked if the helicopter could stop for a ground shot of the arch, and I was told they would. My flying budget had already been reached, but it's on my list to return and get that shot. Sunrise would be best for this subject.

The Arch, Purnululu National Park

Magnetic anthills in morning fog

Magnetic Anthills, Litchfield National Park – Northern Territory

One of my favorite subjects in this book—although not widely known—are the so-called Magnetic Anthills in Litchfield National Park, near Darwin in Australia's Top End of the Northern Territory.

The Park has taken to calling them Magnetic Termite Mounds in recent years, which I think is a more correct scientific designation for the creators of these fascinating subjects, but incorrect in the description of the "mounds." They are more like the monoliths in 2001: A Space Odyssey. Angular, straight and man-made in appearance, they are unlike the usual termite mound, which resembles candle wax after melting.

The magnetic part refers to the orientation of the mounds which line up on the Earth's magnetic fields, supposedly to facilitate cooling in this very hot tropical environment. At any rate, they make great photo subjects, and are unlike anything else I have seen in nature. If you are in Northern Australia, I would not miss the opportunity to visit the town of Batchelor, spend the night, and shoot the mounds at sunrise or sunset. The mounds are clearly marked on the map, and please stay on established trails. Visiting in the dry season with cooler weather will be a plus, as morning fog can add an element of mystery to the already alien forms.

The Magnetic Anthills site is accessible by car.

Anthills aligned to Earth's magnetic field

Handprints panel at Major Art, Arnhem Land

Australian Rock Art

The backcountry of Australia is like a wilderness Louvre. Rock art, especially the paintings (or pictographs), can be found in almost every part of the continent and in every state. I've detailed here some relatively easy-to-get-to sites, and some that are far "back of beyond." Some of the petroglyphs and pictographs may be the oldest art pieces done by human beings, while others are repainted regularly by modern day guardians. You will amazed by the color, variety and superb subject matter for photography.

Kakadu National Park, which is a must-see locale for most visitors to Australia, has two world-class and very accessible rock art sites: Nourlangie Rock and Ubirr Rock. Though Nourlangie is open all year, Ubirr may become flooded in the wet season. Both locales have magnificent paintings, including some in the X-ray style, revealing the inner organs of fish and other animals. You can also see 'Lightning Man' the 'Rainbow Serpent', and the delicate Mimi style.

Davidson's Arnhemland Safaris (requires a bush flight from Darwin) takes

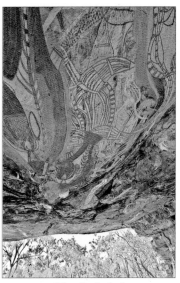

The Cathedral

you to sites like 'Major Art', a huge wall covered in countless colored motifs underneath a huge natural arch, along with many other sites. Again, the dry season during Australia's winter would be the best time to visit this site, which also features a lodge, and is considered one of Australia's finest off-the-beaten-path tourist experiences.

El Questro Lodge, a private ranch in Western Australia near Kunamara, features a boat trip to a large Windjana-style site. Windjana is one of a wide range of distinctly different Australian rock art styles. You may recognize El Questro from the movie, Australia. Hiking trails and helicopters can also take you to the most mysterious Australian rock art of all, the Bradshaw paintings. Some experts date this art at 30,000 years old. Its creators and their culture are unknown.

Kakadu National Park may require permits.

Nearby locations: All three areas mentioned above offer fabulous non-rock art wilderness photography, including water lily-covered billabong lakes, sandstone rock formations, and waterfalls.

Wallaroos pictographs, Cape York Peninsula

Right: The Lightning Brothers

Uluru (Ayers Rock)

Uluru-Kata Tjuta National Park – Northern Territory

I have been to Uluru (Ayers Rock) a number of times over the years and it is always different and always photographically magnificent. On one memorable trip, I was rewarded with a huge bloom of flowers and a magnificent sunrise. Later, a driving rain arrived which brought down flashflood waterfalls on the Rock's walls by the hundreds.

The classic shot of Uluru would be at sunset from one of the designated sunset viewing/photography areas. Find a good one early, because you will not be allowed to go outside this zone, or move from the parking lot area into the fragile desert. Also, you will not be alone. To get something different in this sea of humanity, hope for some great clouds, which are common. Also, since you will be looking southeast for the shot, the cooler times of year from March to September are conveniently best. Recent changes of the sunrise viewpoints have resulted in some less than perfect viewing/photographic opportunities.

Morning Clouds at Uluru

Photography is allowed on sunrise and sunset helicopter flights, which are a good choice. Certain parts of the rock are forbidden for photography, and permits are required from the traditional owners for any commercial photography.

Great Barrier Reef Marine Park – Queensland

As a landscape photographer, the underwater world of the Great Barrier Reef has never been my focus. I think the next time I visit, with good underwater digital cameras so affordable and easy to use, I may experiment with that whole fascinating world. The focus in this book, however, is the landscape above water.

The reef is one of the world's great aerial photography subjects. If you go there, renting a small plane or an helicopter is worth every Australian penny. Though the whole reef is a great subject, the area around Hardy Reef, accessible by aircraft from Hamilton Island, is especially fabulous. Besides Hardy Reef itself, there is the fascinating and perfect Heart Reef, in the exact shape of its namesake. Cook Inlet, with its psychedelic colors and patterns, is also in this area.

Hardy Reef, Queensland

Huge Snag Sculpted by Decades of Waves, Lizard Island

The Whitsunday Islands are the home of tiny slivers of beaches, far from any significant land body, that grow and shrink with the tides. For landscape

Blue Linckia Starfish

photographers, there are also the islands of Lizard, Brampton, and Lady Elliott. These are three favorites where you can photograph deep blue starfish in shallow water. You will find the Blue Lagoon beach on Lizard Island devoid of people, while Whitehaven Beach is considered Australia's most beautiful. To the south, tiny Heron Island is one dense forest surrounded by spectacular white coral beaches. The northern shore is home to nesting sea turtles and, during breeding season (October to April), you'll share the island with 70,000 very noisy seabirds. The resort's submarine and the great snorkeling and diving offer very good underwater photography. Highly recommended.

The locations discussed above are accessible by both air and boat.

The Curtain Fig, Atherton Tableland

The Curtain Fig, Atherton Tableland – Queensland

When thinking about the world's most photogenic trees, strangler figs immediately come to mind. They produce amazing twisted and tortured growth,
each one a peculiar work of nature's art. The Curtain Fig tree in Australia
has gone to singular extremes, creating a fantasy of hanging growth that
resembles an elaborate drapery. Reached by a short walk in the thick jungles of

northeastern Australia, the tree is most easily photographed under cloudy conditions. Fortunately, this is very common in the "wet" season of tropical Australia from November to May. With HDR, it might be possible to work with the extreme contrast of sunlight in this forest, but the subject is surrounded on all sides by huge trees. Under cloudy conditions, I've found the best white light comes when the sun is high, so try to visit the tree around mid-day.

Nearby location: Another great fig tree in the area is the Cathedral Fig. This tree is in a more open area along the edge of the forest and would pick up afternoon and evening light. Though not as symmetrical in its growth as the Curtain Fig, this tree is, undoubtedly, a great photo subject.

Carnarvon National Park – Queensland

The Duchess Natural Arch, Carnarvon National Park

In a country of such great beauty and natural grandeur, this large park in Eastern Australia is my favorite. Some have spent a lifetime exploring this maze of mountains, gorges and amazing geological features. I once saw an old black and white book on the park that was mind-blowing. Natural arches, slot

Tree ferns and sandstone, Violet Gorge

canyons, spring-fed alcoves, prehistoric rock art and giant ferns from the age of dinosaurs are just a few of the attractions here. The wilderness qualities of the park are matched by few national parks in the world.

The easiest entry to Carnarvon Park is through Carnarvon Gorge. The gorge

The Art Gallery, Carnarvon National Park

has numerous trails, including those leading to Moss Garden (hiding the exquisite Violet Gorge), Ward's Canyon and the Art Gallery, one of Australia's finest rock art panels. All these sites are best photographed in shade, so get an early start.

Even though Carnarvon Gorge is the main entrance to the park, the road in can be completely impassable after a heavy rain. During a vigorous wet season, the park may be impossible to reach for weeks. I was chased out of the park during one visit to the Mt. Moffat section by a fall storm. Before my forced evacuation, I was stunned by subjects like Marlong Arch, the Looking Glass, and Kokkaburra Cave. In another very remote corner of Carnarvon I also hiked to the Duchess, a free-standing natural arch, much like Delicate Arch in Utah. It gets great light in the afternoon. I'm sure I'm one of the few Americans who have been lucky enough to visit the Salvator Rosa and Ka Ka Mundi (sounds like a Star Wars name) sections of the park.

Lord Howe Island National Park – New South Wales

Lying about 400 miles east of Sydney, Lord Howe Island is a small but beautiful island with many photographic possibilities. Not part of the Great Barrier Reef, the magic of this small island is the two large peaks, Mount Gower and Lidgbird, that loom above everything. The classic shot of the island is from the lower Mount Eliza looking back toward the ocean and mountains.

The many-faceted shades of blue and green colors of the reefs are best during mid-day, and benefit from a polarizing filter. Using a rented golf cart (cars are not allowed) enables you to get around the island easily and also visit its most beautiful beach, Salmon Beach, with perfect views of the mountains, as a background.

Kentia Palms and Mts. Gower & Lidgbird, Lord Howe Island

Coral Reefs, Mts. Gower & Lidgbird

Most of the time during the summer months, a light plane is available for hire to shoot aerial scenics of the area. For the island itself, get as high as you can to show the whole island and all its colorful fringing reefs. Also, ask the pilot to take you out a few miles to the amazing Balls Pyramid, the world's highest seastack, rising 2,000 feet straight out of the ocean. Midday would be best for the island shot, while Balls Pyramid is majestic at sunrise or sunset. Sadly, with nothing to compare the spire to, the huge rock makes a great image, but its true size is hard to communicate.

Salmon Beach, Mts. Gower & Lidgbird

Tiny Strand of Sand, Rock Islands Nat'l Park, Palau

OCEANIA

Moreaki Boulders at sunrise

Coastal Rock Formations of
the South Island – New Zealand

On opposite sides of New Zealand's South Island, two distinctive geologic formations provide substantial and unique landscape photography opportunities. The Pancake Rocks of Paparoa National Park are the coastal expression of a vast interior of spectacular and rarely photographed limestone canyons and rock formations. Guided trips inside these little-known but stupendous locations are widely available. The Pancake Rocks themselves are a drive-in location at the national park: beautiful wedges of ocean-sculpted limestone that look only slightly like the breakfast food. This West Coat location is best at sunset, with overlooks that afford magnificent vistas down the coast.

Sculpted Limestone, Paparoa Nat'l Park

With little to stop the wind and waves as they travel around this part of the Southern Hemisphere, the gales here can be very strong. I couldn't use my 4x5 camera and had to downsize to the 6x7. Over the mountains and rivers and through the woods, you will find yourself at the small town of Moreaki on the East Coast of the South Island, where a short drive will take you to a magical area of natural globes, or concretions to be more precise, that have eroded from the headlands and now litter the beach like ponderous beach balls. A low tide with sunlight at dawn is best. Don't expect your subjects to be the same each time you visit. Many huge round boulders I shot in the late 1980's were sunk fairly deep in sand in 2007.

Mitre Peak morning reflection

Milford Sound, Fiordland National Park – New Zealand

My memories of Fiordland are intimately tied to my family. With my wife and children, we braved days of pouring rain to stay in our camper van on the shores of Milford Sound. For trekkers, Fiordland is well known for the Milford Track, but for most people, Milford Sound on a clear summer day, an anomaly, is the goal. I didn't know how lucky I was to have the sky perfectly clear and the Sound without the tiniest ripple as I set up my 4x5 view camera, just a few hundred yards from camp. The only drawback was the constant biting of sandflies, which, except in the Southern Alps, plagued us for our entire three week trip. The bites of these horrid insects didn't heal quickly, and my children, especially, were covered in red bites for weeks after our return home. If you plan to visit in summer, you should consider some kind of mosquito hat. The pests were plentiful and could always find a way into the camper.

Besides shooting from the shore towards Mitre Peak at sunrise, the other charms of Milford Sound involve countless waterfalls—including some of the highest in the world—when, not if, the rain comes. Some of the largest plunge directly into the Sound. These can be seen and photographed on the boat tours. The most vigorous rain storms come in the summer months. To get a different take on Milford Sound, try winter when the road is rarely closed; there are more clear days, and snow can reach down to ocean level. Best of all, there are no bugs.

Milford Sound is accessible by car. Cold winters and cool summers are the norm in Fiordland. Some services are available.

Other photogenic fiords worldwide include the world's only desert fiords on the Musandam Peninsula in Oman. Imagine the ocean with coral reefs, surrounded by desert walls thousands of feet high. It's so reminiscent of Lake Powell in Utah and Arizona that you have to keep reminding yourself you're on the ocean, not an inland lake. Though the Musandam fiords are best seen by boat, there is road access to beautiful viewpoints.

Lupine curving along a creek near Mt. Cook

Lupine of the South Island – New Zealand

Though not a native plant, lupine produce one of the world's great wildflower displays in the mountain valleys of the South Island of New Zealand. If the scenery looks familiar, much of the region was used as a backdrop for the Lord of the Rings Trilogy. The cast often stayed at the town of Twizel. This is a good location for viewing and photographing the fields of lupine that take over the lowlands each December, a few weeks before Christmas.

It's not uncommon to have a field of lupine, acres in size, with colors of every shade for a foreground, with the snowy peaks of the Southern Alps behind. Aoraki/Mt. Cook National Park is also nearby, and the glacial blue waters of Lake Tekapo with the snow-clad peak make a great combination. Don't look for lupine in Aorki/Mt. Cook, as they have been removed as weeds. Another hot spot for the flowers is along the highway back to the east coast through Fairlie. Arthur's Pass is also a location for good blooms.

The flowers will be gone shortly after the new year, as they have a short life span. On a trip I made in mid-January, I found none of these engaging flowers.

South Island lupine are accessible by car.

Lupine fields & stream

Nugget Point Lighthouse – New Zealand

Perched on the southern end of South Island, with nothing but thousands of miles of ocean until Antarctica, Nugget Point Lighthouse has geographical significance. It is also a scenic treasure. With the leading lines of the trail guiding your eye up to the tiny structure, and the Nuggets sea stacks to the right, I can't think of a more beautiful lighthouse setting in the world.

Lighthouse at Nugget Point

After an easy drive from beautiful Dunedin, it's just a short walk to the view of the lighthouse. Sunset is the preferred time, as sunrise will create a shadow on the Nuggets from Nugget

Point itself. With light shining directly on the Nuggets at sunset, you'll have the best opportunities. In summer, with the sun in the south, the headlands behind Nugget Point do not block the sun, and therefore allow good side lighting. Weather changes quickly here and this location is often windy. Make sure your camera doesn't blow over—you may want to use your pack as a tripod weight—and be prepared to make several visits to capture good sunset light.

Lupine in various extraordinary colors line the road in early summer here, making great foreground for ocean views along the way to Nugget Point.

Along the Upper Navua River, Fiji

Viti Levu's Waterfall Canyons – Fiji

The fact that Fiji has dozens of stunning beaches is no secret. Lesser known are the jungle canyons that plunge down from the mountain heights to the sea on Viti Levu Island. They are unique in the world, with dozens of waterfalls cascading down the walls of the narrow gorges.

Accessible only on river trips, the native guides have contracted with American river tour companies to offer one of the world's most beautiful and photogenic short river trips. To photograph the waterfalls at their maximum, arrive during the summer rainy season, when daily downpours swell the small rivers and send the waterfalls down into the canyon depths. I did a trip on the Upper Navu

River and counted over fifty major waterfalls. Some were major cataracts, while others were like giant fire hoses shooting down the slot canyon portion of the trip. Take your tripod, of course, as the boat stops at some of the higher falls in the 300-400 foot range. Since the walls of the canyon make stopping at the narrows section of the trip impossible, you'll have to shoot from the boat in this area. Obviously, a water-proof backpack or camera is a necessity.

The same copious rains that charge the waterfalls also make the roads to the put-ins sometimes treach-erous. The rainy season is also the time of typhoons. For these reasons, you might want to plan several days to shoot this subject. There are worse things than hanging out in Fiji in January, right?

Falls on Upper Navua River

Yasur Volcano – Vanuatu

Yasur is described as the world's only drive-in volcano. Getting there is a bit of a long process, but it's well worth it. I suggest you fly to Australia first, and then take the Qantas flight to Port Vila, on the island of Efate. There are a number

Eruptions of Yasur Volcano at Sunset, Tanna Island, Vanuatu

of nice beach hotels there and from that point you can take the short flight to Tanna, home of Yasur Volcano. Stay at the White Grass Ocean Lodge, run by friendly Australians, who will arrange your trip to Yasur. Since they require a three night stay, I suggest you plan to visit Yasur on all three nights. Both malaria and dengue fever can be found here, and although the Lodge's location next to the ocean helps mitigate the problem, take your own precautions to avoid mosquitoes.

The trip to the top of the volcano takes about two hours. As you approach, you'll see a large lava dam with some water pouring over it. During heavy rains, this can turn into a raging river, making the visit to the volcano difficult. Coincidentally, it also becomes one of the world's most photogenic waterfalls, with hundreds of ribbons of water pouring over the natural obstruction. Visiting in the dry season would reduce the chance of seeing and photographing this wonder. At the same time, the dry season reduces the likelihood of disease and the trip to the crater is easier. Perhaps the answer is to visit at both times of the year.

Yaser Volcano at Sunset, Tanna Island

Once you've made it to the parking lot, there's a steep uphill climb to the rim of the volcano. Sometimes gasses and mists rising from below obscure the view—another reason for multiple visits—but usually walking a short distance around the crater affords a clear vista. The amount of noise and constant tremors around the volcano zone can be quite unnerving. They were for me. After a short time, however, my fear subsided as I became mesmerized by the semi-trailer size rocks being blown thousands of feet in the air from below. As darkness descends, the show becomes even more spectacular. Horrible concussions are followed by huge bursts of thousands of flying red lava chunks streaking through the darkness. I suggest a series of 10 second exposures, or even 30 second shots to capture more than one eruption. Although Yasur is supposedly monitored continuously, sometimes it goes crazy—ramping up the size of its eruptions, considerably. Visitors are kept off the mountain when this happens. Although no one has been killed there for 14 years, and a New Zealand team actually climbed down into the crater recently, Yasur is unpredictable and dangerous.

To stand on the rim of Yasur Volcano, though, is a chance to experience and photograph one of Mother Nature's most violent and beautiful events.

Honeymoon Beach, Rock Islands Nat'l Park, Palau

Rock Islands National Park, Palau – Micronesia

This beautiful national park in Micronesia is better known to divers than photographers. I journeyed to Palau to shoot aerial photographs of the Rock Islands (hundreds of small islets covered in green), but the local airplane was temporarily down for repairs. With my planned shot impossible, I moved on to other opportunities the island offered, and there were many. Remember, whether you travel half-way around the world or shoot in your own back yard, your photography plans are not going to always materialize. It's great to be flexible enough to search for alternate scenes and ideas.

In this case, I was fortunate enough to come back with several great shots by renting a boat and exploring the Rock Islands by land rather than air. I found strands of beautiful white sand only a few feet wide, with turquoise waters all around. I discovered great beaches like Honeymoon Beach that I shot by wading my 4x5 and tripod out into the ocean, 20 feet or more from

Honeymoon Beach Afternoon

shore. I found downed World War II planes with their wings still sticking out of the ocean at low tide, and a magnificent arch with sea water underneath, that provided a frame for the islands.

Also, while on Palau, don't miss the lake of freshwater non-stinging jellyfish that you can swim with. With modern-day digital underwater cameras, this can be a magnificent photograph.

Guides are necessary to adequately explore the Rock Islands.

Rock Islands Arch, Palau

Beaches and Waterfalls of Upolu Island – Samoa

What's in a name, anyway? Labelled after a romantic film that was shot here, Return to Paradise Beach is Samoa's finest. Names have actually had a big effect on inspiring me to visit a location. They're part of the ethos of that place—and the trick becomes trying to capture the magic of the name in the image.

The beach itself is best shot in midday, but the sand is so white there, it really gave me problems with exposure when shooting film. HDR would be ideal to tame the dark aquamarines and blues of the sky with the extreme white of the beach—one of the whitest in the world. My composition included the length of the beach and the grove of palms at the far end. You can be the judge as to the success of the image, shown here.

Return to Paradise Beach, Samoa

Left: Sopo'aga Falls & Rainforest, Mulivaifagatola River, Samoa

The island of Upolu has at least six major waterfalls, all ensconced in some of the greenest jungles I have ever experienced. Fuipisia and Sopo'aga Falls are very close to together and in good proximity to the road. Tiavi Falls is a long thin thread. Because of the thick jungle, photographers are forced to shoot from a few cleared areas where the falls can be seen unencumbered. The water flow in the falls is best during the wet season, lasting November to March.

Fuipisia Falls & Rainforest

American Samoa National Park, Ofu Beach

Great beaches are wonderful subjects by themselves. When they have a beautiful backdrop, they are elevated to the sublime. Ofu Beach fits this category as well as any beach in the world, and it's in an American National Park.

Just south of the equator, Ofu is part of the chain of islands that make up American Samoa, an American protectorate. The tidal wave of 2009 did not affect the park, and all facilities are open at this writing. Though temperatures don't change much through the course of the year, summer is very hot and humid and definitely more rainy.

On the island of Ofu, a short distance from the pleasant lodge there, it's a good chance you'll have Ofu Beach to yourself. The idea here is to shoot down

Morning light at Ofu Beach

Sunset light at Ofu Beach

the miles of beach to the spiky mountains in the distance, and although I prefer sunrise, sunset also works well. For shooting the beautiful turquoise water, midday light is best.

Several other islands of American Samoa offer beautiful tropical island landscape opportunities. Tufu Point on Ta'u Island is a great view at sunrise, and Tutuila, the main island, offers some interesting seastacks.

Bora Bora – French Polynesia

The classic atoll shape of Bora Bora, its remarkable inner lagoon, the center island with volcanic peak, its picturesque interior and fringing reefs all combine to create the world's most beautiful small island. There may be prettier islands in some corner of Fiji, or in some remote part of Micronesia, but I doubt it. Even the name's fun.

Bora Bora is easy to get to, but expensive unless you elect to camp, which is a possibility here. A cruise is also an option because a berth on most cruise ships will set you back far less than a Bora Bora hotel. The best light to capture the countless hues of blue in the water appear during the midday sun. There aren't any great beaches here, so your focus will be on the landscape, as you try to capture a little of the Bora Bora magic.

Ancient Polynesian 'Marae', Bora Bora

Probably the most remarkable scenic photos of the island are captured from above in a helicopter, where you can achieve a sense of wonder for what the island is. As mentioned elsewhere in this book, you should fly with a group tour to save money, shoot through the bubble and use a polarizer to cut glare. Many helicopters have windows which open wide enough to use up to a 16mm lens. And remember, an outside seat is best. Not all helicopter pilots will go high enough to see the entire island. This is something you might ask about before you book your flight. Chartering a helicopter will solve this problem, but again, it's not cheap.

Besides the amazing waters, I kept coming back to the interesting center peak. Though often bathed in clouds, the mountain ties the island together. One great foreground for the peak at dawn is the remains of a Polynesian temple, located along the road that rings the island. Not much is left except the lava walls, but they are evocative and feed into the King Kong mystique of the island.

Nearby locations: The island of Moorea is made up mostly of

Aerial view of Bora Bora

mountains and is very picturesque. Particular areas of interest include Cooks Bay with tall peaks ringing the water, and Belvedere Lookout at the end of a curvy road which penetrates the heart of the island. Spiky peaks appear to the west of the lookout, above a deep valley. This is definitely a morning or sunrise shot.

Cathedral Spires, the Marquesas Islands – French Polynesia

I initially saw these peaks on the opening scene for the television series, Survivor: Marquesas. Several of the Survivor seasons have provided me with ideas about places to visit around the world. I'm really not into the show, but the folks who shoot the landscape imagery for the series do excellent work.

Certainly the spiky Cathedral Spires are unlike anything in the South Pacific, rising 4,000 feet right out of the nearby waters. Located on very small Ua Pou Island, there is no official viewpoint, or way to hike through the jungle to get a new perspective. I walked along the road near the hotel, one of the few places to stay on the island, and found a good vantage point there. The Spires (there are about seven on Oave Mountain) were at least partially obscured by clouds during my entire visit.

Nearby locations: Other islands in the Marquesas harbor some wonderful photographic subjects. On the main island of Nuku Hiva, helicopter flights allow you

Cathedral spires of Oave Mountain, Ua Pou Island, French Polynesia

to see and shoot the Vaipo Waterfall—the highest in the South Pacific at 1,148 feet. The falls come down a line of cliffs that is very reminiscent of the beautiful volcanic ridges of Kaua'i. On Hiva Oa Island there are a number of carved deity figures with a slight resemblance to the famous Easter Island Moai statues.

Moai statues at Rano Raraku, Easter Island

Rapa Nui National Park, Easter Island – Chile

Easter Island is another location I would really like to visit again. I found it to have great tropical light, and the legendary Moai statues are consummate subjects. Although wintertime (summer in the northern hemisphere) can be somewhat rainy and cold, January in the austral summer can be a great time to visit, with tropical clouds and brief rain showers.

Vehicles are for rent on the island, and even though the place is small, the many statues are too far to walk to in the hot tropical sun. One exception is the Moai on the western coast (facing east) right near the town. Other great statue sites include the row of seven at Ahu Akivi, just north of town. These make a great panoramic image.

Left: Moai statues, Ahu A Kivi, Easter Island

Moai Statues at Rano Raraku

By far the most amazing setting for the Moai is Ahu Tongariki. It is a great sunrise location with more than a dozen statues backed by high volcanic cliffs and the ocean. A number of shots are possible here, including a wide angle panoramic of the entire grouping to telephoto scenes of the statues with the setting sun. This amazing scene is a recent addition to the park, being restored in the 1990's. You may need a four wheel drive vehicle to get there if roads are bad or washed out.

All these Moai have been restored in recent years, but if you want to see Moai in their natural state, the nearby Rano Raraku quarry is the place to go. Plan to spend at least one sunset here, as there are dozens of heads in excellent shape covering the area below the quarry hill. Some are standing tall, while others are tilted or on their backs. If you're lucky, you'll have great clouds like I did every day. You may also be alone as I was, except for some horses, making for a great photographic and inspirational experience. Don't forget nighttime here. Using the fabulous Southern Milky Way and light painting, it's marvelous.

Besides the Moai, there are several other scenic locations on the island, most in proximity to the national park office near the cliffs where the "Birdman" rituals take place and the Rano Kau Volcano crater. Walk to the cliff's end, and you'll find a rock with large birdman petroglyphs you can use as foreground with seastacks far below. Morning is the best time for this location.

Guides are useful but not necessary.

❖ ❖ ❖

The Matterhorn reflected in a tarn, Swiss Alps

EUROPE

Redbud tree & the Palace of the Council

Ephesus – Turkey

Although technically not part of Europe, this location is culturally and logistically European and is a major stop for Mediterranean cruises.

Following the axiom that the best Greek ruins are outside of Greece, Turkey has a treasure trove. Ephesus, the largest and most famous, is an extensive area that could require several visits. Don't even think about taking your tripod into the site, however, as Turkey's rules about tripods are as Draconian as Mexico's. I had special permission to enter with mine, but I still sat waiting outside, along with a British film crew who were none too happy with the Turkish bureaucracy. Finally, I was allowed to enter, although I was accosted by guards every five minutes who were amazed to see I actually had a permit.

I found the Library to be the most interesting building at Ephesus. It faces southeast, so it's best in the morning. If you visit in spring there are a number of redbud trees on the grounds that add a splash of color to the ancient ruins. My favorite ruin in Turkey, the Temple of Athena at Priene, is a lesser known site, but is in a fantastic setting with a mountain behind it for a backdrop. Facing south, this huge monolith is side-lit during spring and summer, and would have more direct sun in winter. Priene is open for both sunrise and sunset photography. Permits may be required here.

Santorini Island – Greece

Firmly in place as the most beautiful Greek Island, Santorini is famous for its sunsets over the white-washed buildings that tumble down its volcanic slopes. For the fabled end-of-day scene from Oia—the most scenic location on Santorini—walk to the western edge of the village and find a good view over the ocean. The Photographer's

Oia at sunset

Ephemeris is a good tool to obtain information on where the sun will set. There will probably be a lot of people around for this event, but I found my perch earlier in the day to give me a good combination of sea, sun, and Santorini. I returned long before sunset to set up my camera. Using a GND filter on the sky, I waited to shoot until the sun hit the marine layer above the ocean and would not generate flare. HDR would also work well for this. With no clouds, when the sun was down, I packed up. This puzzled many onlookers who commented that I waited all that time and was leaving early. I explained that I really preferred a shot with the sun, and not just a bald sky.

Another classic shot is the blue-domed church of Oia. In keeping with my oft-used technique using two points of interest, I included some bright red geraniums as a foreground. If you're in Oia in spring, look for great flower fields for foregrounds at the base of the village. Telephoto scenes of the white town and the dark

Geraniums & Blue Dome

The cliffs of Imerovigli, with Oia in the distance

slopes of Thira are also excellent choices and there are countless opportunities for detail shots while walking up and down the maze of pathways along the cliff. Thira's cliff faces the south, meaning light on the cliff would be better in the winter months.

The Sanctuary of Athena at Delphi – Greece

Few Greek Temples are placed in magnificent mountain settings like the Athena Temple at Delphi. When I was there, tripods were not allowed anywhere on the site. The Athena Temple however, arguably the most photogenic of all, was left unguarded and open to anyone.

High ridges thrust up all around the shrine, adding a great background to the site at just about any time of day or season—although entering the grounds as late or early as possible is advantageous. Winter would be the optimal time to visit, when snow might cap the surrounding peaks. When I visited in late spring, the limestone peaks were covered with a blanket of greenery. Note that this ruin is downhill from the main area of Delphi and might be missed if you're not looking for it.

A permit may be required here and a tripod is allowed only occasionally.

Sanctuary of Athena, Delphi

Meteora – Greece

Besides the quaint monasteries that are nestled among the soaring rock formations of Meteora, the natural landscape there is one of Europe's most spectacular. Welded tuff pinnacles reach for the sky, covered in spring and summer by verdant vegetation.

Highways weave in and out between the rocks, and just after leaving nearby Kastraki, a trail leads into a half-dozen large pinnacles, with numerous opportunities for image-making. Heading east on this road are viewpoints for the line of rock forms that stretch east to west. Several pullouts allow expansive views, and many wildflowers grow in the area in spring

Spires of welded tuff at Meteora

Monastery at Meteora

making great foreground. Light direction from these scenic viewpoints is good except in the winter when the formations become backlit. A large mountain range to the south of Meteora makes a great backdrop to the whole area in winter, since it is often snow-covered.

Continuing on the road, it's easy to get excellent images of the half-dozen monasteries either isolated, or as part of the majestic natural environ. You can pick up another James Bond landscape here at the Agia Triada Monastery, perched on a thin rock tower. In the morning with the distant mountains covered by snow, you can use a longer lens to crop out the city below. The perched monastery is one of Europe's most dramatic scenes. Summer also works here, but the snow will be gone. The Rousanou monastery is best situated to include a large number of huge rock forms with the buildings. With a longer lens again, this is best done in late spring or summer. The deep greens covering the hulking rocks complement the distant blues and red morning light.

The Valley of the Temples, Sicily – Italy

The Valley of the Temples set off with its centerpiece, the Temple of the Concord, matches any Greek ruin, anywhere.

My attempts to shoot there with a 4x5 are illustrative of the kinds of trouble I had before I switched to digital 35mm with high ISO and lens stabilization. At this ruin, I was accosted by four plainclothes policemen before I had my camera even set up. I was told to "just leave". The Temple of the Concord is not open for sunrise or sunset shooting anyway, but I stayed at a hotel right on the grounds of the ruin. Before dawn, I strolled around the hotel trees and lawns trying to see if there was a sunrise shot from the gardens there. As I got closer to the ruin I saw the hotel gate to the ruin wide open. I quickly walked up to the ruin, set up my camera, and shot as dawn broke and the moon set. I rapidly continued shooting, fearful that I would be arrested at any time. My only defense, if caught, was that I had not passed through any locked gates. Perhaps the same trick will work for you?

This site is accessible by car and all services are available. Tripods are not allowed.

Nearby location: An image of Segesta Ruin, situated all by itself along the highway from Palermo, would best be captured at dawn. Using a telephoto lens, position yourself along the small road that climbs a hill directly across from the ruin.

Temple of the Concord & Setting Moon

Eruptions of Stromboli Volcano

Stromboli Volcano – Italy

Photographing any volcano carries risks, but the Stromboli Volcano makes a spectacular photo subject. The island itself is like a garden and very beautiful, with plants of all kinds growing profusely in the volcanic soil. No one can visit the volcano without a guide, so make arrangements for this as soon as you arrive by ferry from Sicily. On occasion, Stromboli does act up, and the island may be evacuated. This is rare, however.

Your guide will call for you a few hours before sunset to make your way up the trail to the volcano. Several hours and thousands of feet later, you'll arrive at the main viewing spot as dusk approaches. Strombolian volcanic eruptions, named after this volcano, are nearly constant, so you'll only have to wait until dark to begin shooting. Don't bother carrying wide angles up the cone, you'll need 100mm or longer lenses to shoot the fireworks style eruptions from the safe distance you must maintain. Longer exposures are great for combining several eruptions into one shot, and for getting the trails of the molten rocks shooting up into the sky. Try using higher ISO to get some stars in your shot with the lava trails. Eventually, it will be time to leave, but instead of a trail, you slide down the loose lava gravel on the back side of the volcano in mere minutes. Sometimes it seems you're almost skiing, and as I slid down the mountain an almost full moon rose out of the Aeolian Sea. I could almost picture Odysseus and his boat plying the moon-dappled ocean, as I smelled the roses of the village below.

The Amalfi Coast – Italy

Staying on the glitzy Amalfi coast can be an expensive proposition, so many visitors base themselves in Naples, Pompei, or Sorrento, and visit the Amalfi on day trips. There is no substitute for spending a few nights there, however, if you want to photograph the amazing towns and cliffs when the light is at its best.

Spread out over two impossibly steep hills separated by a ravine, Positano is the crown jewel of the Amalfi coast. Coming from Naples or Sorrento, there is a good panoramic view from the Belvedere della Madonnina—all buses stop here—but the most spectacular shots are from the east side of town looking west toward the steep hill with its dozens of houses clinging precariously to the cliff-side. Although there are some good shots from the beach—perhaps using fishing boats as a foreground—the best views of the hilly town are from hotel terraces above the beach. Buca di Bacco and Marincanto have great terraces from which to shoot the town with the Church of Santa Maria Assunta in the foreground to create depth. Another good spot is from the road out of town toward Amalfi. Crowds are smaller in May and September and this would be a good time to go.

Stormy weather on Amalfi

Positano dawn

Amalfi has the only long pier along the coastline, allowing you to get a panoramic view of town with striking limestone cliffs in the background. For even better shots of the cliffs, hop on one of the tourist boats that ply the coast.

High above Amalfi, Ravello has superb views of the coast from a belvedere at the end of the Villa Cimbrone. Try including some of the Roman sculptures to add depth to your shots.

Nearby location: Just off the coast, the island of Capri attracts similar hordes of tourists, with even more glitz. The coastline is spectacular all around the island. The Grotta Azzurra, or Blue Grotto, is a major attraction and worth the complexity of the logistics; first you take a mid-sized boat, then you transfer to little row boats that take turns whisking two or three of you inside the cave. The Grotto is flooded with blue light reflecting from the entrance on the crystalline waters. It's hard to keep things level, so use high ISO and take lots of shots, checking your LCD often.

The Monuments of Rome – Italy

Rome is not a place where tripods are welcome. It's best to try to handhold all your shots, as you will almost certainly be asked to take your tripod down and go elsewhere. I personally had no problem on the sidewalk near the Colosseum, or at the Spanish Steps, but it was another story at the Forum. Fortunately, I had just completed a good shot there with dramatic light and a threatening sky.

The Colosseum

Photographing the Colosseum from the sidewalk, shooting toward the west, is great in the afternoons of late spring and summer. I have seen a number of quality night images from there, which must have been done with tripods. I can only believe the police are not harassing photographers there too often. Remember also, in the spring there are throngs of visitors present during the daytime.

The police were also unconcerned about my presence at the Spanish Steps. Hopefully they will ignore you. Arriving very early in the morning in April might afford a good image of the steps with the profuse azaleas adding some color. There will be fewer people as well, since nobody in Italy seems to get up too early. I don't know what it is with Mediterranean countries and tripods at historic sites, but it seems to be an area of wide concern for authorities. Greece is the most difficult in this regard, but Italy is not far behind.

Tripods are allowed only at specific locations.

Azaleas at The Spanish Steps

Skyline of San Gimignano

Tuscany – Italy

The American public, possibly due to books touting the romantic character of the area, is in love with Tuscany. Please refer to the Florence description, herein, for more photography suggestions.

My favorite scene in Tuscany is the Towers of San Gimignano, one of Tuscany's most famous hill towns. The angular steeples and campaniles there glow at dawn when seen looking toward the west, and have a luminescence that belies their antiquity. Just hope when you arrive that the spires are not covered with scaffolding and cranes. On my trip a few years ago, there were few of the Tuscan hill towns not obscured by large cranes. One exception was the huge Castle of Monteriggioni, a large walled town surrounded by green fields and wildflower meadows. One of the great things about Tuscany besides the food and wine are the detail images that abound. Pay attention to the little things in Tuscany and you'll come back with some intimate landscapes that say as much about Italy as your big scenics. One example is the small grove of cypress trees on a green hill near San Quirico d'Orcia. Every photographer that drives by is compelled to shoot this scene. Another such scene along the road from San Quirico d'Orcia to Pienza is the small chapel of the Madonna de Vitaleta, which is best at sunset.

A few years ago, the Italian government tried to control photography in Tuscany like the English are doing now, but indications are that their rules were impossible to enforce and they have backed off. That's not to say a policeman might hassle you, although none bothered me and my 4x5 while I was there. I can almost guarantee that if you're shooting at dawn, no one will be around to bother you.

A permit is technically required in Tuscany, but this is not enforced.

Cypress cluster in early morning sun

Florence – Italy

Two subjects in Florence really inspired me for outdoor photography. Of course the city is much more than photo subjects, and it's easily possible to photograph between museum visits and gastronomic indulgence.

Florence's Duomo

Ponte Vecchio

Certainly the front facade of the Duomo captured with a wide angle lens (streets here are narrow) is a colorful and structural delight. I waited in Florence several days for sunlight to hit the Duomo façade, with good clouds behind. The sun needs to be high overhead to accomplish this, as there are tall buildings all around to block the light. Late spring or summer is best. I was shooting with a 4x5 at the time, and the detail that I crave so much is a big part of the interest in this shot. That same kind of detail can be approached digitally by using Photomatix Details Enhancer in the Tone Mapping setting of their HDR program. Obviously this is accomplished by software, but the end result can match a 4x5 original in detail. Also, Topaz, a Photoshop plug-in, has a details enhancement mode that does not involve HDR.

A great sunrise shot of one of Europe's most historic bridges, the Ponte Vecchio, can be achieved by arriving early and slipping down to the "off limits" boat dock on the south and west side of the bridge. This puts you right at water level for an excellent reflection at dawn. Fortunately, at that time of day, no one seemed to care I was there. The bridge will pick up the most light around the equinoxes, and you will want to use a GND (graduated neutral density filter) or HDR. Although I have been questioned about my tripod in many Italian locations, no one ever bothered me in Florence or greater Tuscany.

Cinque Terre National Park – Italy

Originally fishing villages, the ultra-picturesque towns of Cinque Terre (literally 'five lands' in Italian) are perched on the plunging cliffs of the Italian Riviera, above the Ligurian Sea. The best access to the area is by train, which makes stops at each of the five towns. Most visitors stay in Monterosso, where a trail begins that hugs the tops of the cliffs with great views to the towns below. In May, this trail is covered with wildflowers, providing foreground companions to the many-colored buildings stacked and squeezed into the small villages nearby.

Cinque Terre is an afternoon/evening subject, as the towns face mostly west. Though Riomaggiore is appealing with its tiny harbor full of multi-colored boats, my favorite town at sunset is Manarola. The latter has a large cliff across from it, offering a great vantage point to shoot the whole town at sunset. Don't forget the intimate detail shots here like clothes hanging on the line and charming doorways. I know you will not forget to enjoy the seafood, pasta and wine.

Cliffside Town of Manarola at sunset

Varenna at dawn

Lake Como – Italy

If Lake Como hadn't already been world famous, George Clooney's villa and a top Las Vegas hotel would certainly have contributed to put it on the radar. By now, few people haven't heard of Bellagio—the epitome of the northern Italian lake town, with its opulent villas surrounded by Neoclassical statues, cypresses, and dripping wisteria.

If you're going to stay a few days on the lake, Menaggio is a good base of operations: it has more hotels, affordable places to eat, and things to do. Menaggio proper doesn't offer great shots of the lake, but it has the best access to Villa del Balbianello (which appeared in Star Wars - Episode 2) and the ferry will take you to Bellagio and Varenna in less than 20 minutes.

Arguably, the best street scenes are in Bellagio, but some of the better villas and most interesting views of the lake are in Varenna. Villa Monastero and Villa Cipressi (the latter a hotel) are especially great for photography.

Both Bellagio and Varenna are packed during the day, but Italians are late-risers and tourists want to make the most of their expensive hotel rooms: you'll have the place to yourself early in the morning.

Nearby locations: Although somewhat overshadowed by their prestigious neighbor, Lake Maggiore, Lake Lugano, and Lake Garda offer very similar scenery and architecture. Lake Maggiore is only 25 minutes from Milan's Malpensa Airport. It has a number of very photogenic small islands and great views of the Alps in its northern part. Some of the villas rival those on Lake Como, especially Borromeo Palace on Isola Bella. The Monte San Salvatore funicular near Lugano (in the Swiss part of the lake) offers spectacular panoramic views.

A 1-hour train ride from Varenna puts you at Milano Centrale (a sight unto itself) and a quick subway ride brings you to the center, where you can photograph the remarkable Duomo (cathedral), do a bit of shopping, and enjoy a latte while watching the best-dressed crowd in the world.

The Italian Riviera – Italy

The Ligure Coast, best known as the Italian Riviera stretches from Monte Carlo to La Spezzia, with great cities like San Remo, Rapallo, and Genoa (of Christopher Columbus fame). Three locations stand out for photography: Portofino, Santa Margherita Ligure, and Porto Venere. Porto Venere has a row of great old buildings lining up the waterfront and a convenient jetty to photograph them. Loaded with flowers, Santa Margherita is a large, convivial town with an expansive bay and the most beautiful buildings of the Riviera—decorated with 'trompe-l'oeil' frescoes. It also makes a convenient base to visit Portofino.

Few visitors dare tackle the impossibly narrow road that follows the coastline and I don't recommend that you do. Instead, just enjoy the flat 3-mile walkway along the blue Mediterranean waters. With an early start, you'll be there with plenty of time to photograph the spectacular harbor in the best morning light. You can try a bird's eye shot from the church (but big yachts often partially obscure the view) or simply walk to the end of the jetty, which gives you a perfect view of the colorful buildings reflecting in the water. There are also good shots from all the cafes near the yacht dock. Be sure to be in position shortly before sunrise. You can return (or go) by bus or cab.

Portofino harbor in early morning.

Hilltop Village of Peillon

The Hilltowns of Côte d'Azur – France

Provence gets all the attention in Southern France, but there are a number of beautiful towns perched high on the cliffs of this area that I find to be some of the best photo subjects in Europe. Peillon, a beautiful town very close to Nice,

Peillon

glows with an inner light at sunset in the early summer. Facing west, it should get good light in late day, all year. A telephoto is great for shooting from the road below, while a wide view shows the rugged canyons and cliffs surrounding the town.

To visit amazing Saorge, you will have to take the freeway almost to the Italian border on the east side of Monaco. It's a short drive up the curving road where the cliffs climb immediately to dizzying heights, right from the ocean. From below, I composed the improbably-perched town with a beautiful mountain stream in the foreground. This required walking down a small embankment. The town itself appears l-shaped from the road below, but basically faces west. Another great image is achieved by shooting across the town from its east side in the morning, toward higher peaks in the distance. In the winter, the peaks may often be snow-clad.

I'd like to offer some caution here. As mentioned in the introduction, the only crime incident I've had in my extensive travels occurred in the town of Nice, the gateway to this area. Be wary of your car rental company, which may be in league with the criminals, and get out of Nice as fast as you can. Also keep your guard up as you photograph and travel in the Côte d'Azur region. A story makes the rounds about thieves robbing an entire photo workshop group in the area. Most people have no trouble, but please stay alert.

Boats & shops in Cassis, Provence

Provence – France

Provence holds a special place in the world's imagination. The cliché involves vast fields of lavender and quaint summer cottages under perfect blue skies. Provence is a photography subject of subdued grandeur. Certainly the lavender fields are great in mid-summer, but the spring poppy fields are much more color-ful, albeit less widespread.

Lighthouse & cliffs, Cassis

My favorite town is Roussillon, known as the 'Red Village' which is most beautiful in the winter from the small forest viewpoint to its south. In the distance, the snowy Alps foothills add a great backdrop. Outside Roussillon, beautiful orange rock formations can be found. The light seems to always be good here: clean and clear.

Sometimes the Provence Coast is forgotten, but it's here the most amazing landscapes of all are hidden. The fabulous Calanques are inlets in the white coastal limestone that harbor hidden beaches and great spires, arches, and other rock wonders. The best way to shoot and see this area is by boat form Cassis, the very picturesque port town with a cool backdrop and lighthouse. Outside the town, huge cliffs climb directly out of the ocean and glow orange at sunset. The town was immediately recognizable to me from the movie

Poppy Fields in Provence

Right: The Calanques

French Connection. Be careful in this area, however. It is the only area I have visited where I have been mugged, and I would avoid Nice and Marseille like the plague. It's preferable to fly into a smaller town in Provence, such as Aix. Also, the drivers here seem highly aggressive and less than sane. On the positive side, the food is magnificent, and buying produce from local vendors (wash carefully) provided strawberries and fresh peas unlike any I'd had since my Iowa boyhood.

Sagrada Familia Church, Barcelona – Spain

Some people may not like Sagrada Familia, but I think, even in its less than complete state, it is one of the world's most amazing architectural achievements and a fabulous photography subject. My goal in shooting the Sagrada was to

Sagrada Familia – Gaudi's unfinished masterpiece

show the eight amazing towers that have been built so far. To do this, I researched viewpoints in the area and found one at the Hispanos 7 Suiza Apartments a few blocks away. The Apartments staff welcomes photographers and the location is far enough north to give you a great side view of the towers from the roof of the building. When I visited, it was open at all times to guests. Outside of hiring a helicopter at thousands of euros an hour, I don't know how else to attain this viewpoint. Further, the apartments are quite close to the small park in front of the church which can provide some foreground and framing trees. If enough photographers visit the Hispanos 7 Suiza, I might get a free room next time.

The Sagrada Familia from the front is an afternoon and evening shot, with the tallest towers and the main entrance facing west. Unfortunately the night lighting of the church is not very conducive to photography. The lights come on after dark, and are not colorful, hence my night shots didn't work well at all. I digitally removed the many cranes around the site, but left the scaffolding as it looked interesting. I hope to return someday when the promising central tower and four more on the south will be added. What a shot that will be!

Tripods are allowed only outside the main church grounds.

The white city of Casares

Casares – Spain

Believed to be named after Julius Caesar, Casares is literally not on the map. You can find signs that point to it as you travel on the Costa Del Sol east of

Gibraltar, and as you get closer, your GPS may (or may not) include it as a destination.

The most scenic of the "white towns" that dot the coastal mountains in the Andalucia region of southern Spain, Casares is mostly situated on an east-facing slope. To find the best view of the town, travel up from the west and pass several restaurants on the top of the ridge. A large parking area, not heavily used, has a viewpoint where you'll want to end up. In the morning, the white 'casas' are directly lit as the sun moves down the cliff from the top. In the evening with the sunset behind, the white town tints blue, reflecting the sky above. Employ HDR or a GND filter here to mitigate contrast. There are very few hotels in the area unless you wish to commute from the more hectic coast. I stayed at the Hotel Hermitage, just a few miles from the overlook.

The Park & Palace of Pena, Sintra – Portugal

Near Lisbon, one of Europe's most whimsical castles is surrounded by a beautiful forest. The castle itself is not ancient, but is unusually colorful in yellow, blue, red, violet, and other shades, while the forest is home to everything from Sequoias to South Pacific tree ferns. The park staff is unusually welcoming to photographers, one of the reasons I have listed Pena in this book.

The best view of the castle is had in the morning from the statue of the warrior,

Pena Palace

a group of granite rocks that allow you to get above the tall, dense trees. There are also many deciduous plants in the forest that would provide some of the best fall color in Europe. This touch could nicely complement an image of the castle. In spring, during May and June, the castle is surrounded by huge blooming rhododendrons. Avoid weekends as the crowds and traffic are nearly unbearable.

Nearby location: The Sintra coastline has great seastacks, granite boulders, and sea cliffs that photograph well at sunset.

Chambord Castle

The Loire Valley, France

A car GPS will come in handy in the Loire Valley to guide you to the great castles that dot the beautiful rolling landscape there. First among them for me is Chambord Castle, which is beautiful not for its location, but for its many towers. It's not Disneyesque in the slightest, but still ranks as one of the world's great castles. The grounds here are open for sunrise and sunset, and my favorite view is from the southwest at sunset around the equinox. Chenonceau Castle is a delightful shot with its arches that cross the river and reflect in it. Try to catch Chenonceau as early as possible in the morning but it is not open for sunrise. At Montsoreau Castle, it's possible to cross a vineyard and come out on a cliff high above the castle on the sunset side. This also allows a great view of the river and the countryside beyond. Chateau d'Azay-le-Rideau has the best moat for reflections in the morning. You will need at least a 14mm lens to take it all in. The chateau is not open at sunrise and HDR or a GND filter is recommended here.

I can honestly say with all the photography I have done in France, I have never been troubled for permits, asked to leave, threatened with arrest, or accosted in any way. I believe photographers should reward countries that welcome them with return visits, and if possible, avoid those like England and Italy who are trying to make photography more difficult.

The castles of the Loire Valley are easily accessible by car.

Mont Saint-Michel – France

The offshore religious fortress of Mont Saint-Michel is unique in the world. Surrounded by extensive tidal flats—these can prove dangerous when the tides come in quickly—the famous abbey is often the brunt of some of Europe's worst weather, especially in winter.

I rented a nearby French farmhouse in November and went to shoot at the ocean every day. It took a week to get a good reflection and sunrise. The rest of

Mont. St. Michel, Normandy

the time I enjoyed nearby restaurants, walked the nearly abandoned countryside during midday and napped as the hard winter rains pelted the roof. It was my idea of what a great photography trip should be: one great subject, lots of time, plus good food and lodging. The only stress came from driving even short distances on French highways. Since the only safe place to shoot the Mount is south of it on the nearby shore or causeway, the light is best during the winter months.

Nearby locations: The seaside town of Honfleur is not overly colorful but the elongated harbor buildings are unique and the wooden boats add interest. At the White Cliffs of Etretat—sort of a French version of the White Cliffs of Dover— you'll find a huge sea arch and trail along the cliffs with chalk-white seastacks.

Notre-Dame Cathedral

Paris – France

There's a lot to shoot outdoors in Paris, so I've condensed this entry into three of the best-known sites: the Eiffel Tower, the Arc de Triomphe, and the Notre Dame Cathedral. I photographed all these locations with a tripod and had no trouble with the authorities. I understand that shooting the Eiffel Tower at night is no longer allowed however, because of lights that were added in the last ten years. Though the Tower itself is in public domain, the lights are copyrighted,

and they can't be photographed without a permit. Shooting at sunrise and sunset sans lights is OK, and I had very good luck in the pre-dawn hours with no one around.

The ideal time of year to shoot all of these landmarks is in the winter months. The front facade of Notre Dame faces southwest, for late afternoon light, while the huge Trocadero park in front of the Eiffel Tower is situated on a southeasterly slant towards the monument. Weather is more unreliable in winter, but visitors are also fewer. A sunset shot of the Tower from the west would conversely be best in midsummer, and it's possible to incorporate the River Seine in the shot from that direction.

A quiet evening on Monet's Nymphea pond

Nearby location: Monet's Estate in Giverny is only an hour outside Paris by train or car. The gardens are of special interest to photographers for their spectacular flower displays and the Nymphea Pond, where the famous Impressionist loved to paint. The place is mobbed from mid-April through October, but some photography workshops offer a chance to photograph after hours.

The Eiffel Tower at dusk

Spring Tulips & Flowers, Keukenhof

Keukenhof – The Netherlands

Photographers with tripods and professional looking equipment are sometimes not welcome in privately-held locations such as gardens. Keukenhof Gardens in the Netherlands is one of the major exceptions. During my several days of shooting there with my 4x5 kit, I was made to feel sincerely welcome. These gardens, just a short drive from the Amsterdam Airport, are a color shooter's dream in

Keukenhof gardens

every way. Tulips, of course, are the main draw, and they delight the senses with every hue you could imagine. Near the ocean, early morning shooting often involves fog, which seems to add even more color saturation here. Check the Garden's website for the peak of the spring bloom, which is usually mid-April. Try to avoid Easter, as the crowds are sometimes huge. Keukenhof also has a fall tulip bloom.

Other photogenic European Gardens include Brockhole Gardens in the English Lake District, ablaze with rhododendrons and azaleas featuring mountains for background. Muckross Gardens in Killarney National Park in Ireland has some of the largest rhododendrons I have ever seen. Also with a good mountain background plus a castle, the blooms at Muckross come in May. Powerscourt Castle and Gardens, also in Ireland, has been home to many movie productions and has wonderful May tulips. A different kind of garden with pumpkins, squash and other vegetables makes a great foreground for beautiful Rivau Castle, in France's Loire Valley. Rivau faces south and is best in September at harvest time. All the above gardens are accessible by vehicle.

Vianden Castle – Luxembourg

The large, stately castle of Vianden straddles a high ridge of the Ardennes Mountains near the German border in Luxembourg. Approaching the castle from above on the highway coming from the west offers numerous vantage points at several pullouts in the afternoon. Down below in the quaint village of Vianden, a small river offers morning reflections, gardens and flowering trees in spring. It would be a good idea to scout some of these out before your morning session. The Battle of the Bulge was fought not far from here in snow during World War II, and the castle itself would be a fabulous subject after a winter snowfall.

Castle at Vianden

Mont Blanc & the Alps – France & Switzerland

Mont Blanc in France is such a huge presence that it can be seen and photographed from neighboring Switzerland. The Valle d'Aosta, through the tunnel into Italy, also offers great views of the famous mountain, especially with castles like Saint Pierre in the foreground.

The Chamonix Valley is a good place for a base to photograph this area. A number of chair lifts and gondolas operate year round to take you high into the ranges where you can shoot until sunset and walk down. One of the Alps most beautiful scenes is the reflection in Lac Blanc of the rugged Les Aiguilles Peaks,

Mt. Blanc reflected in lake, French Alps

located a little east of the Mt. Blanc massif. Local postcards record this stunning place, and Art Wolfe has a famous image of it. A gondola takes you to within three miles of the small lake, and if you have clear, calm conditions, it would be worth shooting sunset there and walking out with a headlamp or even spending

Annecy's Palais de l'Isle

the night. My luck was not so good in a week of photography—another reason I prefer desert shooting—but I did find a small lake just along the highway in Chamonix that featured a great reflection of Mount Blanc itself.

Nearby locations: The Palais de l'Isle, in the town of Annecy, is a highly photogenic medieval building in the middle of the river in the downtown area. It is a striking scene at dusk, when the street lights are on.

The Matterhorn – Switzerland

As a boy growing up in Iowa in the 1950's, my main conduit to the outside world was Walt Disney, whom I idolized. In 1959 Disney released a still critically acclaimed movie called Third Man on the Mountain, a mostly true story of the first ascent of the Matterhorn, which was filmed in Zermatt. On one of my first trips to Europe, I accomplished a long-held dream to see and photograph the peak that had an aura of magic for me my entire life.

I was not disappointed, and spent five days in Zermatt, waiting out weather and trying to find the best locations to shoot the iconic mountain. In the process, I happened on a local festival exhibiting alcohol abuse on a scale that I have not seen before or since, but that is another story. The Matterhorn can be shot from Zermatt itself, but in my quest to always get closer to my subjects, I took the Gornergrat glacier train to the alpine plateau with great views of the Matterhorn and all the surrounding Alps. One stop was beside a small tarn that perfectly reflected the mountain in the morning: one of the best shots to be had of the peak. Riding the Gornergrat train from Zermatt to the top of its track offers thrilling views into the Italian Alps and amazing alpine wildflowers for foregrounds. A good scenario for photographing the mountain is to stay at one of the hotels along the train route, higher up the mountain. From there it feels like you can reach out and touch the Matterhorn. Five days spent there would be enough to witness many moods of this world-class natural subject.

The Matterhorn reflected in a tarn, Swiss Alps

Lauterbrunnen Valley – Switzerland

A miniature Yosemite in the shadow of the Jungfrau, the Lauterbrunnen Valley has the requisite glaciated wall and waterfalls, but with the added touch of quaint villages and a waterfall "inside" the cliffs. Staubbach Falls, at 1,000 feet tall is a wonder all by itself.

The walls here are less warmly colored than Yosemite, and hold a definite blue cast. Lupine is omnipresent, and this, along with the church tower, make great foregrounds. Seventy-one other waterfalls are known in the valley, definitely edging out Yosemite in sheer number. To see these falls at their most magnificent, late April or May after a snowy winter is best. Lauterbrunnen also has its own Glacier Point-like lookout called Männlichen. A cable car, operating all year, will take you to this stunning view of the valley and the Jungfrau.

Lauterbrunnen Waterfall

The Obergletscher Ice Cave, Grindelwald – Switzerland

Ice caves form in many glaciers throughout the world, though they are somewhat dangerous to visit for obvious reasons. The Ice Cave at Obergletscher in Bernese Oberland is open to the public every summer. Spikes are employed occasionally to stabilize the cave, which is a short walk from the parking area. This ice cave does not require crampons or other glacial exploration gear.

Inside the ice cave, you enter a blue world like an ice version of a slot canyon, except all the light is coming from the opening and not from above. Most ice cave shots work best by reaching the back of the cave and shooting toward the opening. A midday visit is good, as you will want as much light as possible to bounce into the cave. The "wrinkled" texture of the cave is really the subject here, forming rhythmic patterns on the cave walls and ceilings. This is a chance to photograph ice that is very old and has a more clear blue, ice-cube like quality. The ice can sometimes be extremely blue.

Other safe photogenic ice caves include the Eisriesenwelt Werfen in Austria, near Salzburg. Though more a deep cave with artificial lighting, this ice cavern

Left: Lauterbrunnen waterfall & lupine

Ice cave inside Obergletscher Glacier, near Grindelwald

claims to be the largest in the world. Iceland probably has the most amazing ice caves on the planet, but they come and go and can be very dangerous. A tour to Lofthellir Ice Cave is less dangerous because the ice is forming underground in a stable lava tube. Possibly the best ice cave in the world is Crystal Cave in Iceland—if it still exists—which should be visited in winter when chances of cave collapse are at their least, and with a guide. Mendenhall Glacier near Juneau has some great ice caves that can be explored with a guide in summer.

Neuschwanstein Castle – Germany

Most Americans gained a perception of what castles should look like from Walt Disney. He got his ideas from Neuschwanstein! As castles go, Neuschwanstein was built quite recently (19th century), so there's not much wear and tear.

I spent several days photographing the castle, waiting for good light and clouds, and searching for good viewpoints. The Mary's Bridge view, which I finally chose, is great during mid-morning in late spring and summer. From the bridge you are looking north to the green plain and the lake, which is very scenic. What I really wanted, though, was the scene found on many postcards showing the castle front taken from a high ridge directly opposite. This is a great view of

Neuschwanstein Castle, Bavarian Alps

the fortress with the beautiful Bavarian Alps beyond. At times, I try to recreate shots I've seen in a different or unusual manner, and I can usually find the spot where the photo I've seen was taken. I find nothing wrong with using the photos of others as a starting point.

Certainly, many have done that with my work. In this case, however, after hiking and climbing every inch of the area I thought the viewpoint must be located in, I just couldn't find it. Ironically, I later learned from a workshop attendee that guides from the nearby town will take you there.

The Castle is a great subject throughout the seasons, but especially with fall color or snowfall.

Neuschwanstein Castle from the bridge

Val di Funes & Dolomite Peaks

Val di Funes, the Dolomites – Italy

Called the jewel of the Dolomites, the Val di Funes is possibly the most beautiful drive-to spot in all the Alps. It's so easy to get to: only three miles from the A13 freeway just south of Austria, and you're there. The Dolomite Range is as sharp and craggy as any mountain range in the world and the whitish rock seems to glow at times. Like the Sierra, they truly are a "Range of Light."

Of course, the mountains are only part of the story. There are the green meadows and the perfect churches that make this one of the most idyllic scenes in the world. Any internet search will pull up pages of stock images, wallpaper, and posters. This is a relatively new phenomenon, by the way. When I first photographed this subject, I received emails from all over the world wanting to know the location.

My image here took about four days. I arrived in late spring when I knew the greens of the valley would be strong and there would still be snow on the peaks. There was also the three day rain storm that I waited out, and benefited from afterward, as it left lingering clouds and crystal clear air. Since the mountains face northwest, May is the perfect time for sun position and polarization angle.

Why polarize in this digital age? In this case, the polarizer took the sheen off the lush green grass.

When I looked for my shooting location, I found a large rise on the north end of Santa Maddalena that put me up slightly above the whole scene. I had to drive a little, and then hike up a grassy knoll. With a sky full of clouds, I was also given spotlighting, my favorite weather condition. At times, the spotlight would hit the church and the mountains, and I used a GND filter to hold back the bright sky. Currently, I would probably count on HDR for the same effect. I continued shooting this basic set up for hours, moving around the same small area. On the following day, I included flower fields with the mountains, eschewing the standard scene. I've seen some amazing winter images of Val di Funes and any place this beautiful will always have something to photograph.

Buses can take you to a network of easy, well-marked trails in the high-country above the Val, offering great close-up shots of the Geissler Range. You can hike leisurely from hut to hut, where they serve refreshments (or even a meal). It doesn't get any better than that.

Nearby location: Tre Cime di Lavaredo is another photographic icon of the Dolomites, accessible by car from the Cortina d'Ampezzo resort town. It is best at sunset from near the car park.

Venice – Italy

Suggesting you can get great images in Venice seems superfluous. The entire place is a photographer's dream and it will not disappoint. The center of attention is the Piazza San Marco, and staying near there will give you a chance to shoot many great subjects. Photographers are drawn to the boat dock near the Doge's Palace where dozens of gondolas covered in blue are lined up along the

Yellow Gondola, Venice

Canal in Venice

shore. With HDR or a GND filter, this can be a great sunrise location. The Basilica San Marco is also perhaps best at dawn when it is still lit (artificially) and the dawn glow begins to show in the sky behind. I also recommend detail shots of the amazing marble around the front entrance.

Basilica San Marco, Venice

Other intimate landscapes abound in medium close-ups of colorful gondolas and other wooden boats parked along weathered walls of great character. The best idea is to ride around in a gondola or wander the maze of streets. Photo ops will present themselves everywhere. A map can help locate bridges for canal vantage points. The nearby Rialto Bridge is a great location to shoot up or down the canal, with colorful Venice buildings on either side. Shooting from along the canal, the Rialto Bridge itself makes an interesting subject at dusk when the lights come on. The Accademia Bridge also provides a timeless view of the Grand Canal looking east toward the Basilica of Santa Maria della Salute. This last image is best captured at sunrise.

Nearby location: If you like Venice, you'll love Burano. Just 40 minutes by water bus from Venice, the small island known for fine lace is the ultimate candy shop for photographers. Canals here are lined with buildings of every color imaginable and you will have a ball exploring the endless compositions. Overcast days are probably best here to saturate the color.

Burano canal

Plitvice Lakes National Park – Croatia

Part of the karst landscape of Eastern Europe, Plitvice Lakes is probably the prime example of karst lakes and waterfalls in the world. All the elements of the beauty of limestone erosion are present: waterfalls, Caribbean blue lakes, natural

Blue-green waterfalls at Plitvice Lakes

Plitvice lakes & waterfalls

arches, and caves. Plitvice packs a lot of beauty for such a small size.

Waterfalls cascade through steep-sided canyons over travertine dams and also crash off the rims. When you're in the middle of all this, it seems as if waterfalls have taken over the world.

The prime area is around the Big Waterfall, which intersects an area of smaller falls coming down the main canyon. The classic shot is from the western side of the canyon at a viewpoint accessible by climbing in and out of the canyon (the main entrance is on the east side) and shooting upstream from high up. From this viewpoint, it's possible to include two blue lakes with the waterfalls that drain them. Midday with sun—a tough time to shoot the white water—brings out the amazing blue-green colors of the lakes. A polarizer is also a great tool to increase the exposure time on the falls and take the sheen off the lakes, allowing pure strong color to shine through.

I visited the park in late April during a period of heavy rain—an event that caused them to swell mightily. As the rains tapered off so did the falls, so there is some luck involved in seeing and photographing them at their best. I saw many images that convinced me that the park would be great in winter and fall. Since the water comes from underground, it has to be very cold to freeze the falls completely, and the area gets a lot of snow. Snow images with good waterfalls are a little unusual, so it might be worth braving the off-season to catch them. Also, fall color here is some of the most beautiful in Europe—another palette of color to add to the blue waters.

Photographers with tripods are welcome and the park is open during daylight hours. To walk into the park to shoot dawn, buy a two-day pass to cover you on the next morning. There are no restrictions on being in the park at any time as long as you have purchased a pass.

Lake Bled – Slovenia

One of the Alps' best photo subjects is not in Switzerland or Austria as you might expect, but in beautiful Slovenia. Lake Bled is hardly a wilderness location, but with the Julian Alps in the background, a castle on a nearby cliff, a church steeple on an island and glacial blue waters, it has a reputation as one of Europe's most striking locations.

Church on Bled Island

It is possible to photograph Bled Island and its church from shore, often with swans in the foreground, but a more exciting scene is reached by a trail that begins near a campground at the lake's eastern end.

One of your biggest challenges at Lake Bled is parking your car near this location. So, if possible, book a hotel nearby or take a bus. The trail climbs steeply to two overlooks above the lake: one lower and easier to get to, while the other is higher and more expansive. In both spots, you may have to work to see the lake through the trees, and be very careful of crumbling rock as you climb up. This route is not particularly difficult, but is not for those who fear heights or lack scrambling skills.

The shot works best here in the late afternoon of spring and summer when the high sun angle helps saturate the blue glacial waters of the lake. I visited this location in May and was disappointed at the lack of snow on the Julian Alps, which would have created a stronger image. Perhaps April would be better, and the crowds would be smaller. Also, ticks carrying encephalitis are common in this area and may be less active in the cooler weather. I found many great snow shots on postcards, and I believe the area gets a lot of storms. Climbing up to the overlook then, however, would be very dangerous.

Lake Bled & the Julian Alps

Morning Fog at Hallstatt

Hallstatt – Austria

The Austrian Alps contain a wealth of scenic wonders. To settle on one is difficult, but the small town of Hallstatt has been called the world's most beautiful lakeside village. A World Heritage Site, Hallstatt is located at the western edge of Hallstättersee and the base of the Austrian Alps. Besides the 'Sound of Music' style Austrian buildings, the beautiful church tower sets off the whole scene.

I searched all day for the best location to shoot at dawn, when I thought the lake would be quieter, the light direction better, and reflections more interesting. It took several days of waiting out spring rains to gain these conditions. Finally I was in place at dawn with my 4x5, but this time it looked like heavy fog that had settled in overnight would ruin everything. Fortunately, the strong early-summer sun quickly burned off most of the fog, leaving just a long tendril of the stuff reflecting in the still lake. Once again, some advance scouting and a little patience were well rewarded.

I have seen photos of the village late in the afternoon that work also, but not as well. Under the even light of cloud cover, the colorful shops of Hallstatt make a great scene of their own.

Russian Orthodox Churches – Russian Federation

The number of fantastically-colored and historic wooden churches in Russia must be considerable. In a cruise from Moscow to Saint Petersburg you'll see many pass by, usually too fast to grab your camera unless you're constantly vigilant. A cruise is probably the best way to visit the wooden Church of the Transfiguration on Kizhi Island. With 22 onion domes and its wonderfully aged wood, it has withstood fierce North Russia winters since 1714. Next to it is an older, though smaller Lazarus church from the 1200's. If you select a cruise for your visit, you won't be in control of when you stop at the island, though morning seems to be a favored time. The church sits basically on a north south plane, and the north side of the church is the most photogenic. It works well for side-lighting from the east in the morning and the west in the afternoon. Cruise ships usually spend two hours here. A bed and breakfast on a nearby island might allow visiting the church during magic hours, but taking a small boat out on huge Lake Onega would frighten me. I would recommend visiting only aboard a large ship.

St. Petersburg and Moscow have many churches, but the Spilled Blood Church in St. Petersburg and the famous St. Basil's Cathedral on Red Square take the prizes in my book. Spilled Blood makes a great reflection in a nearby canal with a very wide lens at sunrise in summer. The color in the mosaics and baroque details of the building are wonderful also, while St. Basil's onion turrets are a riot of color. The east side of St. Basil's can be shot with a tripod from a large nearby

St. Basil's Cathedral, Moscow

Church of the Transfiguration on Kizhi Island

parking lot, but shooting across Red Square with a tripod was not allowed on the day I visited. Though I came to Moscow in summer, a more atmospheric time might be the winter with its continual snow. The psychedelic onions of St. Basil's would make an interesting contrast to the snow-covered urban tundra.

Lysekil – Sweden

Photographers are drawn to quaint seaside villages the world over and several interesting examples are highlighted elsewhere in this book. Lysekil, with its rocky setting and colorful buildings, is the most beautiful such location in Sweden.

Lysekil is the Malibu of Sweden, as it has been home to movie stars including Ingrid Bergman. Surrounding the church steeple, the perfect houses are colored red, yellow, blue, orange and white, all with orange roofs. Lysekil is very busy on weekends in the summer, and parking is at a premium. On my visit there, I found a relatively high domed rock perch to shoot eastward during the afternoon. Sunset may tint the many colors of the buildings with red, so afternoon shooting works well.

Nearby location: The highly impressive Tanum rock art sites reveal the life and beliefs of people during the Bronze Age. Access to the area is unlimited, and the

Left: St. Petersburg's Spilled Blood Church

The quaint, colorful seaside town of Lysekil

various panels make great subjects at dawn and sunset. The figures were re-paint-ed some years ago to increase visibility. It's a testament to the Swedish people that the unprotected art has not been vandalized for 2,600 years. The site across from the visitor center is situated to pick up sunrise light around the summer solstice. All the rock art is surrounded by birch forests, which make beautiful backdrops in autumn. Tanum certainly qualifies as one of the world's great rock art sites, and easily one of the most photographer-friendly.

Nyhavn – Denmark

The harbor area of Copenhagen is lovely on its own, but Nyhavn, a canal which reflects colorful shops in its waters, is one of Europe's best photographic possibilities. Located in the heart of the busy city, it's also very accessible since it's only a few blocks from waterfront hotels.

To obtain optimal reflections, the waters become very still on late spring or early summer mornings (probably around 4:00 AM, perfect if you have jet lag), with the light direction ideal when shooting from the east side of the canal. At that time, there will be fewer people around and the shops will not yet be open. Nyhavn can

Colorful buildings in Nyhavn

be shot from east to west in the afternoon and evenings, but boat tours and huge numbers of people descend on the shops and restaurants then. Remember that reflections are best with a sunlit subject and water that is in open shade; so when the sun clears the buildings, as it does quickly, your best opportunities are done. After capturing the post card views, look for interesting abstract patterns in the colorful reflections.

Nyhavn harbor

Sunrise on Reine, Lofoten Islands

The Fjords – Norway

I love the comment in 'The Hitchhikers Guide to the Galaxy' when an architect of Earth says, "I won an award for Norway."

The weather forecast for my Norway trip showed two weeks of rain, a common condition in summer. Though I thought about canceling or postponing the trip, I'm glad I didn't. Everything was green, and the waterfalls, some of the highest in the world, were really cranking. My first fjord visit was to Lysefjord. It was quite a long walk, and I climbed up to a viewpoint called Pulpit Rock. Expect hordes of people; it's Europe after all. Sometimes you have no choice but to include the crowds, and people add a sense of scale. With sun coming and going, I waited for a break in the clouds from the viewpoint. The color of the Fjords is important and always seems to be best with strong overhead sun. Clouds are an important part of my work both as subjects and modifiers of light. Sunrises and sunsets were almost always obscured in my time in Norway. I enjoyed only one good sunset in the two weeks I was there

Geiranger Fjord, longer and with many waterfalls is really the best in this area and easily accessed by car from Bergen. I arrived as a heavy rain abated, and noticed an ephemeral waterfall a short distance from the road. I always like to get closer to my subject. In this case there was no trail, just a steep ridge that led to a small platform big enough for a tripod. I estimated the waterfall at 500 feet high, and I took some shots including a boat to provide scale. The lighting was overcast, except for a few gaps that allowed the sun to spotlight the water. I could also see the Seven Sisters Waterfall in the distance. Later I chartered a boat from Geiranger to shoot the falls from ocean level. For an additional vantage point, I followed a rough trail that climbed the wall opposite the falls. I attempted a shot I had seen in the past of the Fjord from a very dangerous looking viewpoint on the car switchbacks that climb out of the head of the Fjord. This was closed, however. I spent about four days at Geiranger, altogether, and you will want to give this location as much time as possible.

Hardanger Fjord boasts a 600 foot waterfall. You'll probably want overcast light for the shot, and that will be easy to come by.

The Lofoten islands, located above the Arctic Circle, have spectacular fjords. The most photogenic of the bunch is the Kirkefjorden by the small fishing harbor of Reine, close to the tip of the farthest island—all are linked by bridges making the trip easy with a rental car. The classic view of the fjord from Reine, with the tall conical-shaped mountain jutting out in the background, is best shot at sunrise from the entrance to the village. Another great shot can be had from Reinebringen Peak, far above Reine; the trail is very steep and can be dangerous when wet. Getting up there for sunrise with a headlamp takes almost an hour. Lodging in Reine consists almost exclusively of fishermen cabins and is impossible to find without reservations in July/August. Early September is a good time for photography and general travel in Norway, which has great fall colors.

Nearby location: I loved the fantastically sculpted shore rock called Kannesteinen near Ålesund. Perhaps because it was the only time I saw the sun at sunset during my entire trip. It's a small eroded feature, but very unusual and worth the trip.

Geiranger Fjord

The Standing Stones of Stenness, Orkney Islands

The Orkney Islands – Scotland, U.K.

This small island group packs quite a few great possibilities into a small package. It's also a very pleasant place to go in summer, when temperatures are great and there's a good mixture of sun and clouds.

The Yesnaby cliffs and seastacks are highlights among some of the best seascapes in the British Isles. The North Gaulton Castle is one of the most photogenic stacks in the world, with a very thin eroded base. If you like lichen, like the great photographer Eliot Porter did, you'll find some of the largest and most colorful lichen-covered rocks I have ever seen. The Yesnaby Castle rock formation actually has a sea arch in its base. All these features are on the west side of the island, so sunset is the preferred time to shoot them. Besides these geologic wonders, the Orkneys in July are blessed with large fields of wildflowers.

The Old Man of Hoy is another great seastack on the nearby island of Hoy. To reach it would require a boat, or riding the ferry and pursuing a long walk—well worth the trouble. The Orkneys boast at least two ancient standing stone areas which are part of the Megalithic Orkney World Heritage Site. They include the incredibly thin Stones of Stenness, which have defied gravity for thousands of

Right: Yellow Lichen along the Orkney Islands coast

years, and the Ring of Brodgar, featuring 60 stones in a circle. Some of these are over 18 feet tall, weighing many tons. Ancient alien theory would tell us...

The Callanish Stones, Isle of Lewis

The Callanish Stones – Scotland, U.K.

Standing stones are a common and mysterious sight in much of the ancient Celtic homeland. France actually holds the largest site in Carnac, with over 3,000 stones. My favorite are the Callanish Stones on the Isle of Lewis, Scotland. They stand on a high promontory next to the ocean where light can play beautifully on the individual monoliths. Many people think it ranks second only to Stonehenge in England, as a magnificent ancient monument.

Although the trip is a long one by plane, car, and ferry-boat, once you arrive you'll not find the crowds of Stonehenge. Also unlike Stonehenge, you will have access to the site at sunrise and sunset. Increasing visitation is causing more restrictions here, so my advice is to go now before Callanish becomes like its aforementioned sister. I stayed at a nice bed and breakfast right next to the Stones and foraged for several days shooting the changing light. The proximity of the ocean increases the chance of bad weather, so you may want to schedule extra time here to make certain you get some good light. It's a beautiful and relaxing island, so enjoy it while you wait.

With digital equipment, I think the Callanish Stones would be great at night, something that didn't work too well with film and a 4x5 camera. A stitched-panoramic would work well here also. A lesson to bear in mind: as technology changes and new techniques become available, revisiting these great sites can offer new opportunities.

Photographers visiting the United Kingdom should be advised that in the last few years, the National Trust, which functions like the National Park Service in the United States, has clamped down on photography without a permit, including photography that appears on Facebook or Flickr. Though there are some rumors they've backed off a bit, please be warned that there is a concern here. The World Wide Web provides conflicting information about this subject, and I am not a lawyer.

Old Man of Storr, Isle of Skye

The Isle of Skye – Scotland, U.K.

Among a range of scenic wonders in Scotland, the Isle of Skye comes to mind first because of the amazing reflections I saw there one autumn morning. As I drove back to the mainland, I couldn't determine where the reflection ended and the real thing began. I have seen no better reflection phenomena in all my travels, and I saw a hint of the same on my second winter trip to Skye. For my

photo recommendations, I've picked some sites quite close together that are equally fascinating.

Both the Old Man of Storr and Kilt Rock are north of Portree, about five and ten miles respectively. The Old Man of Storr is actually five pinnacles rising above the ocean, approximately one mile from the coast road. These spires were recently made famous in the amazing movie Prometheus. Though best at sunrise or in the morning, the pinnacles also work in the afternoon. Take care walking up to the area as there are lots of steep inclines and loose rock. Mealt Falls with Kilt Rock beyond is one of the few waterfalls in the world that pours over a large cliff directly into the ocean. Without recent rains or snowmelt the falls may be non-existent. If you can get there with a good flow on a sunny sunrise, however, you will have a great opportunity.

The Scottish Highlands – Scotland, U.K.

Anyone who's seen Braveheart, Rob Roy, the Harry Potter films, or any of the other great Scotland-based movies has to marvel at the Highland landscape. Many of the great Scottish castles (discussed in the next entry) are located in the Highlands, along with waterfalls, snow-capped peaks and countless lakes and ocean inlets. All seasons are great for photography here, including some glorious (although short) days of winter shooting.

The Western Highlands area probably command the most bang for your buck, and the famous Glencoe area is a hotspot with Loch Achtrochtan and Buachaille Etive, perhaps the most beautiful peak in Great Britain. Black Rock Cottage, a favorite subject of mine since my first Scottish trip, can be shot with a looming mountain in the distance. Also near Glencoe is beautiful Grey Mare's Tail Falls. Be careful of the extremely slippery rocks on the way to the falls.

Cottage in the Highlands, near Glencoe

Left: Falls at Kilt Rock

Other lochs (lakes) further afield include the famous Loch Ness with Urquhart Castle offering great reflections. Loch Loyne is also spectacular with good road access and mountain vistas. For high mountain views, nothing beats riding the gondola to the top of Ben Nevis, near Fort William, shooting from the top until sunset and then walking down with your headlamp.

See related entries about shooting in the United Kingdom.

Scottish Castles – Scotland, U.K.

I don't know why I like castles so much. Maybe it's my Disney-influenced childhood, or maybe it's because many are part of great landscapes. I found the largest concentration of castles with good scenery in Scotland. Some look like they were built yesterday, while others are in ruins strewn across battlements usually facing the ocean. The light in Scotland is often akin to the light in Ireland, with sun and clouds coming intermittently to provide constant drama and chiaroscuro.

The best castle of all, used in many movies and even doubling for M's hideout in a James Bond movie is Eilean Donan, surrounded by majestic mountains and the ocean. In spring, prolific rhododendrons work as foregrounds and if you're lucky enough to get snow in winter, there are countless possibilities. A small road near the castle leads off the highway up to a viewpoint looking west over the castle and sound. Since the main highway passes next to the castle, it's always possible to shoot at sunrise or sunset.

Craigievar Castle

Eilean Donan Castle in Winter

Craigievar Castle looks almost new, with its unique compact structure, huge grounds and orange color. Entry to the grounds is controlled and there are many trees making a sunrise or sunset shot impossible. To shoot the castle from the front, be there in the morning, and you may get lucky like I did with a splash of quick sunshine highlighting the castle against a dark sky. Another favorite is Stalker Castle, sitting on its own island in Loch Linnhe. Roads encircle the castle, offering vantage points for all times of day. Winter sunrise with snow-clad mountains behind has given me my best images at Stalker, but I have seen impressive images here taken in autumn with the surrounding hills ablaze with color. Dunrobin Castle, unlike many Scottish castles, is in private hands but welcomes photographers. There is great side-lighting on the castle, seen from the beautiful gardens in the early afternoon in summer. Later in season, the castle is primarily lit from the front. The ruins of dramatic Donnottar Castle cover a promontory surrounded by cliffs on all sides. A small causeway connects the near-island to the mainland. For this photo, the best shot is at sunset near the carpark. In spring and summer, greens cover the area, making great contrast with the yellowed castle and the dark blue, often stormy sky. Since the summer sunsets last hours, gathering your patience and waiting for the sun to blast through is the best strategy. I often wait hours or much longer for good light on my subjects,

Stalker Castle, Loch Linne

but I'm content being where I want to be, doing what I want to do. What could be better, right?

As mentioned elsewhere in this book, the rules for taking photographs of National Trust Areas in the U.K. have toughened considerably and are being enforced. This comes at a time when the number of photographers making any kind of income from landscape photography has hit an all-time low. A ranger at Urquhart Castle on Loch Ness pressured me unmercifully, then quickly changed his demeanor and became my buddy. This schizophrenic attitude toward photographers leaves us never knowing what to expect from authorities, and takes a lot of fun out of a completely innocent activity that helps boost the UK economy in several ways.

The Lake District – England, U.K.

Celebrated by the great English poets, the northern part of England is a land of low mountains and lakes that is reminiscent of the Appalachian Mountains in America. The attractions for photographers are both natural and historic. Beauty here happens all year, so great subjects can be found in every season.

Spring in the Lake District is very special when wildflowers fill the forests, waterfalls are flowing abundantly, the weather is improving, and the gardens are

Right: Aira Force waterfall, Lake District

Boats at Ullswater Lake

filled with chromatic diversity. Aira Force waterfall, famous in poetry and song, has a unique arched bridge at the top, and is a road kill shot. The Castlerigg Stone Circle is a grouping of huge monoliths beneath gorgeous peaks. In winter and early spring at sunset this site is wonderful, although the green lawns of late spring are also appealing.

Most of the subjects mentioned here reside in Lake District National Park, which may be subject to the UK's new aggressive photography rules for National Trust lands.

Brockhole Gardens

Caernarfon Castle

Caernarfon Castle – Wales, U.K.

A huge imposing castle sitting on a tranquil ocean inlet full of colorful boats, Caernarfon is at once majestic and familiar. The finest view, capturing seven towers and massive walls, is seen from across the river looking north to the castle. A park with several viewpoints adjacent to the water is easily reached by bridge, a few miles upstream. The general orientation of the castle walls is south-facing, so the best light for photography is on the short days of winter, at sunrise or sunset. Winter is also a very stormy period on the Welsh coast, and I have yet to see a brilliant sunset image of the castle. In spring rhododendrons can be used as foregrounds. As a National trust site, there may be legal sanctions for photographing the castle without a permit.

Snowdonia National Park – Wales, U.K.

Snowdonia has so much variety and so many great subjects, it's no wonder it makes many "top ten" lists. The park is a combination of natural environments,

Swallow Falls

including mountains, lakes, waterfalls, beautiful coastlines, forests, gorges, and wildflowers. Great castles and decaying settlements round out the list. As a person with Welsh heritage, I couldn't leave it off my personal list.

Snowdonia is often a rainy, stormy place. This adds to the melancholy mood of this mountain kingdom. It's also perfect weather for shooting the great waterfalls like Swallow Falls and the aptly-named Fairy Glen, a lush canyon adorned in mosses and ferns. The Snowdon Mountain Railway, running in the summer, is a perfect way to get up to the high country and wait for good light with a 360° panorama of mountains and lakes. Ride the train up and walk the short, but steep, mile down.

Stonehenge – England, U.K.

Stonehenge lives up to all the hype. There is simply nothing like it! Sadly, however, there is nothing like the set of ever-changing rules one needs to follow to photograph there.

Stonehenge has evolved a lot since I visited twenty years ago. I was then able to take my 4x5 everywhere but right inside the circle. Now, forty feet is about as close as anyone is allowed without special permission, but tripods are definitely allowed on the boardwalk that encircles the stones. Entry to the center of the stones is not allowed during the normal hours, which end long before sunset. When I visited recently in April, closing time was 6:00 PM—not quite magic hour. I captured some good daytime images including clouds and then shot a great sunset from the road with a telephoto lens.

Each morning and evening, up to 26 people are allowed inside the circle by permit. Getting a permit for this is easier than getting one for the Wave in Arizona. Just visit the English Heritage web site and sign up for "Stone Circle Access". I'm sure tripods are not allowed, but since it rains in the U.K. just 30 percent of the time, your chances of getting good light are fairly strong. A fee is charged for this privilege, and you'll be shooting at the best time of day (with other people possibly in your way). Special photography permits can be purchased long in advance for a hefty fee.

Stonehenge

One way around the restrictions is to hire a light plane or ultra-light—there are a lot of these around for viewing crop circles— and shoot the stones from the air at sunrise or sunset. Even accomplishing this, the English government asserts that it owns the copyright of all Stonehenge images, and controls all sales of the images for commercial purposes. English photographers have been understandably upset about this, as it includes all English parks and shorelines. There is a lot of confusion as to what is, or isn't covered in their edict, and there has been some backpedaling due to the outcry. It's definitely a place for serious photographers to approach with caution.

English bluebells, Micheldever Woods

Nearby locations: Possibly the world's most beautiful forest understory wildflower blooms are the fabled English bluebells popping up in Britain's woodlands each spring—a joy to see and photograph. My favorite place for bluebells is the Micheldever Woods. The Woods are open to photographers at any hour on any day, so arriving before dawn or staying until sunset is possible, and desirable. Also, tripods are allowed at Micheldever. Many of the other famous bluebell sites don't allow tripods and are only open on certain days and with limited hours.

The trees at Micheldever are special too—beeches that provide a good environment for the flowers as well as a beautiful background thanks to their warm-colored bark.

In general, the bloom starts in mid-April in the south of England and moves up the island as temperatures warm up. The flowers are usually fairly tough and long-lasting, so you may have several weeks to shoot. Don't expect to see bluebells from the parking lot at Micheldever—you've got to get out and walk through the almost always mucky interior. Though overcast lighting is probably the most common, be prepared for fog; early and late sunset will also work. Since I found the bluebells to be a little patchy, I often used a short telephoto to bring multiple patches into one image.

Durdle Door Sea Arch

Left: Stonehenge stone circle

Sometimes the name of a place is enough to get me excited about visiting and photographing. When I looked into the Jurassic Coast region of southern England, I saw a lot of interesting subjects packed into a small area: sea arches, sea stacks, white cliffs, romantic ruined castles, and some of the best thatched-roof towns in the country. The high point has to be the Durdle Door, a large sea arch that is the symbol of the area. Late spring and summer sunsets are the best times to shoot this great north-facing formation, unless you have a boat. I would avoid this area in late summer and on weekends.

One of Europe's best castles, Corfe, stands on a high hill near the ocean; it has vantage points for both sunrise and sunset. The best view is from the north during the summer, as that angle allows the most ruined towers to be seen. All the small towns in the area have ancient homes with wonderful thatched roofs; you'll come across many of these as you explore.

Giants Causeway National Park – Northern Ireland, U.K.

The volcanic rock formation called columnar basalt is the star at this seaside park on Ireland's northern coast. The geometric shape of the rock is the origin of the name as it appears to be crafted and put into place by man, or in this case the mythical Finn McCool. Naturally, this unique rock structure makes a fascinating subject, and a stellar foreground for the roiling ocean.

Rainbow at Giants Causeway

Right: Giants Causeway & approaching storm

Storm at Giants Causeway

Since this coast seems to always be stormy when I visit, there are a lot of chances to use the weather as a secondary subject. Rainbows and dark clouds with lots of character really add to the scene, and the sun often breaks out for added drama. The causeway area generally faces north, although there are enough breaks in the headland to permit shooting at almost any angle, at any time of year. This is an area ripe for return visits and is open for sunrise and sunset presently, although a new visitor center and parking area have recently been built. On seven trips to Ireland, I have never had anyone question my tripod and big 4x5 camera, even at National Trust Lands in Northern Ireland.

Dromberg Stone Circle – Ireland

In any other place, this stone circle, although interesting in early light, would not be especially remarkable. Throw in the beautiful green rolling hills of County Cork as a backdrop, and you have magic.

I recommend staying at one of the nearby B&Bs that are close enough to the Circle to make driving or even walking easy. Sunrise in spring or summer is best with sidelight striking the stones from the left (or northeast), while you shoot out to the ocean in the west. Shooting this scene at this time of year will also ensure that you have an absolutely emerald green landscape in the distance. To do this, you will have to rise early—another reason to sleep nearby. Perhaps the hardest part of capturing this image is the weather. A sunny morning on the west coast of Ireland is not exactly rare, but it's probably no better than a 50% chance on any late spring or summer morning. This scene really sums up the spirit of Ireland: greens, the ocean, lush farmlands separated by rock walls, and the ancient Celtic culture that seems to hang over everything. Since the ground is likely to be covered in dew, waterproof or Gore-Tex boots are a good idea here.

Drombeg Stone Circle

Ross Castle

The Ring of Kerry – Ireland

Widely accepted as Ireland's most beautiful drive, the Ring of Kerry has a number of exceptionally scenic locations and classic views. Everything you expect of Ireland can be found here including green forests, gardens, lofty mountains, castles, and ancient wonders.

At the very beginning of the route, Ross Castle in Killarney National Park has kept me busy photographing on many occasions. The moat is a perfect reflecting pond on still mornings and evenings, and is accessible at both times. Walking north around the banks of Ross Bay in Lough Leane, you will find ways to combine the castle and the surrounding mountains with a telephoto lens. In early spring or late fall, snow may even be a part of the scene. Another more modern castle is Muckross House and Gardens, a short distance away. In May, the flowers there are the best I've seen in Ireland, especially with the blue-hued mountains to use as backgrounds. At the same time of year, huge rhododendrons explode with thousands of blossoms.

Ireland does not have a large number of waterfalls, but continuing around the Ring you will come to Torc Falls, with the greenest mossy trees I have found

Left: Old growth oak forest, Killarney Nat'l Park

Rainbow at Ladies View, Killarney Nat'l Park

anywhere in Europe. Next is Ladies View, not superb, but great if you can get a rainbow there as I did. My average rainbow count while shooting in Ireland is about five a week.

As you climb up from the Killarney valley and head towards Kenmare, the peaks of Ireland's highest mountains, Macgillycuddy's Reeks, come into view. I always think of I Love Lucy and her maiden name when I visit here. There are lots of wildflowers to use as foregrounds in the summer and snow may provide a different mood at other times of the year. Great hikes penetrate the range with trails to the top of the highest peaks. Kenmare is remarkable too, for the Druid's Circle. The name alone is enough to excite me, even though the rocks are some- what small compared to Ireland's biggest monuments. They are still impressive though, and appear like white mushrooms growing from the greenest field you'll ever see. Use a wide-angle lens here and get as much of the Ring as possible in view. Continuing around the circle you'll find photogenic Irish homesteads and more rocky headlands that are best in the afternoon and evening hours.

Nearby location: The Dingle Peninsula is also a great drive; some even prefer it to the Ring. The town of Dingle is a magnet for visitors enjoying its special atmosphere. It has a busy harbor, very colorful and photogenic houses on the waterfront and main streets, a nice church, and plenty of good pubs and cafes.

Svartifoss – Iceland

Picking which one of Iceland's waterfalls is best for photography is a challenge.
If you love waterfalls, visit Iceland in the spring when melting winter snows meet the tough volcanic rock and form thousands of cascades.
Some are so large that they are difficult to capture, and others drop hundreds of feet into giant cones of ice. My favorite though, and one that seems to be on every tour's itinerary, is Svartifoss. The falls itself is not large, probably no

Svartifoss Falls

more than one hundred feet, but the colors and patterns of the columnar basalt over which it pours are unparalleled. The falls is also notable for being part of Skaftafell National Park, Europe's largest park.

Ice floes in midnight sunlight, Jökulsárlón Lagoon

Jökulsárlón Lagoon – Iceland

I was fortunate enough to be one of the first photographers to capture this natural wonder with a 4x5 camera. Icebergs of all shapes and sizes, prevented from reaching the ocean by a volcanic dike, float around in the lagoon and pose for the camera. Jökulsárlón is so unique, it's been in two James Bond movies! It's truly a must-see and must-photograph location.

I would imagine the lake is frozen over in winter, but if you come in May, June or July you'll be rewarded with hours of great sunrise and sunset light. When I first arrived after traveling by car along the Iceland Ring Road, it was about six in the evening and the entire lagoon was completely deserted. I had some camp dinner, set up my tent, and then began shooting for almost seven hours. Sometimes the clouds obscured the sun, but it would eventually reappear. Finally, I used a GND filter for a backlit shot into a sunset that lasted about an hour.

Right: Ice Floes, Jökulsárlón Lagoon

Ice Floe in June midnight sun, calving from Vatnajökull Glacier

The icebergs were constantly moving a little, so a faster shutter speed is recommended.

Boat tours ply the Lagoon during the day, but it's easy to just walk around the shore and shoot the ice sculptures. Especially interesting are the clear ice pieces, which I believe are the oldest. The sun shines right through them like huge pieces of fine crystal. It was great to have the whole place to myself for so long. Since I visited the lagoon, it has almost doubled in size.

❖ ❖ ❖

Heavy snow at Yaki Point, Grand Canyon Nat'l Park

NORTH AMERICA

Fiord & fog at Western Brook Pond

Gros Morne National Park – Newfoundland, Canada

Reaching the viewpoint above Western Brook Pond, the best vista in Gros Morne National Park, requires advance preparation including adequate camping gear. A ride on a tourist boat and a climb up a steep headland are additional requirements toward your goal.

I suggest you hire a guide, available in Rocky Harbor or Woody Point. You will also need to be prepared for all kinds of weather, especially rain. Extra food is a good idea because the boat that drops you off at the base of the hike also picks you up, and high winds may delay its arrival. Normally, the hike to the viewpoint is just a long, hard uphill trek with 2,000+ feet of elevation gain. When I visited and rain fell in buckets, the trail quickly deteriorated and my guide and I used tree roots to pull

Sunrise at Western Brook Pond

ourselves to the top. Once on the summit, the storm broke but left the canyon filled with tendrils of fog. It was not the look I had envisioned, but actually much better.

Upon reaching the top, there is not a singular ideal spot. Look for a clearing to shoot over the trees. The pond is situated on a northwest-to-southeast angle, so shooting down the water from above will be a backlit situation in summer, with a little better side-lighting in the morning. HDR or a GND filter will be helpful here. Insect repellent and a good tent are both strongly encouraged. The tour boats are very popular here and often fill to the brim, meaning you may have to wait a day or to two to acquire a seat. An alternate means to reach the viewpoint is by snowmobile in winter. The noisy contraptions can drive directly to the overlook. Expect extremely cold conditions and short days, but possibly stunning photos. Permits may be required here.

Lighthouse at Peggy's Cove

Peggy's Cove – Nova Scotia, Canada

The quintessential Atlantic maritime village, Peggy's Cove offers a dramatic lighthouse and quaint fishing harbor, both very photogenic. Just a short distance from Halifax, I acquired more good images of the lighthouse there in a few days than any I have visited. Interesting clouds were always present in the sky and tide

Lighthouse at Peggy's Cove

pools provided calm reflections. Fog was another bonus and turned the sun to a red orb, appearing ghost-like, above the sea. The granite head-land turns orange at sunset and makes a great foreground. Though the location in winter is much colder and wetter—snow is a distinct possibility—with larger waves, any time of year provides good photography at Peggy's Cove.

Nearby locations: The town of Lunenburg is great, chock full of colorful buildings and boats.

New England Fall Color

No place in the world holds a candle to the fall colors of the Northeastern United States, in scale, intensity, and variety of color. Along with the trees is an interesting landscape, besides. Every year is different in terms of timing and strength of the color palette. Fall color forecasts are often wrong and the trees change at different times according to elevation. The first area to turn is the mountains of Maine and New Hampshire, and then much later at coastal locations like Acadia National Park. The alchemy that produces a great fall color season is still a bit of a mystery. I have stayed home when a bad year was forecast, only to find out later it was one of the best. Some prognosticators believe cold nights and bright sunny days during the crucial change period, have the biggest impact.

Probably the most legendary location for great fall color is the Kancamagus Highway in the White Mountains of New Hampshire. Besides great trees, the mountains form a complete tableau of beauty. Add one of the many covered bridges or old red barns and you have a cliché, but a gorgeous one. Remember also that the leaves can be photographed after they fall. Some of my best autumn images are of a waterfall or covered bridge surrounded by a sea of covered leaves that cover the entire forest floor. You will not be alone in New England during fall color season, and the crowds and traffic tend to diminish the experience. Fortunately, most are not out at dawn, which is the best time for trees in morning mist with a lack of wind. Rainy days, which are common here in fall, tend to thin out the crowds and are great times to shoot the many waterfalls in the area surrounded by color. Finding someplace to stay in New England at this time of year is difficult, and booking a room or a campsite a year in advance is sometimes mandatory. Commuting from Boston is not unheard of.

Other areas to shoot fall color: Other states in the eastern US have color rivaling New England. New York is often magnificent, although the Catskills can become

Right: New England Fall color

Clearing Storm, Cadillac Mountain, Acadia Nat'l Park

incredibly crowded on fall weekends. Western New Jersey around the Delaware Water Gap National Recreation Area is a great spot, and often uncrowded on weekdays. In Pennsylvania, World's End State Park has perhaps the best fall color I have seen anywhere, if conditions are right. If fall color is really your bag, following the Appalachian Mountains from Maine to Georgia during September and October would provide endless opportunities for fall color landscapes. I did this once and it was a highlight of my life and photo career.

The Clinton Mill – New Jersey

The Red Mill of Clinton is one of the most photographed locations in the United States, probably due to its proximity to New York City and suburban New Jersey. As an example of a beautiful historic American grist mill, it is almost without peer. Its shape, color, reflecting pond, and waterfall all contribute to an idyllic scene.

The mill building faces northeast and reflects in the adjacent mill pond. During a late spring or still summer dawn, it is a perfect image with strong sunlight. Use a GND filter or HDR to control exposure. If you come at other times, your biggest problem will be finding a parking place. At dawn you should have the spot to yourself, but you need to time your shot so the Mill is lit but the sun has not yet hit the water. A large cliff rises behind the mill, so if you want to incorporate sky you will have to use a wide angle lens. It's easy to crop the sky from the composition if it is uninteresting. To use the waterfall as a foreground, move downstream. A shutter speed of 1/2 second gives the flowing water a silky look without reducing its strength in the image.

Other photogenic American grist mills include Dun's Falls Mill on the Meridian River in Mississippi, which has a large waterfall and aging wood exterior with a lot of character. Also in the South and easy to get to, is the Pigeon Forge Mill just outside Great Smoky Mountains National Park in Tennessee. This mill has a good waterfall foreground, a strong reflecting pond and wonderful aged wood construction. Sunset in spring and fall is best at Pigeon Forge Mill. In the Northeast on Cape Cod, Brewster Mill is very lovely, whether surrounded in spring with wild roses and lush greenery or in winter by snow. West Virginia's Babcock Mill in Babcock State Park is a true gem of the Appalachian Mountains. Winter snow, late spring rhododendrons, and autumn color all compliment its historic beauty.

Spring Morning at Clinton's Red Mill

New York City Skyline

The New York City Skyline – New York & New Jersey

The best place to shoot the skyline of New York City is actually from across the River in New Jersey. The optimal shooting location is Liberty State Park.

Though the Twin Trade Towers which dominated the New York skyline are obviously missing, the other buildings are very imposing and the Hudson River provides a good foreground. Use your car's GPS to locate the park, which is a large area facing the city. There are usually so many visitors and policemen there, it seems very safe for being in such a large urban area. Even after 9-11, I have used a tripod in the park and no one objected. Beware of leaving anything in your car at the parking lot, though, as it is not patrolled and thefts are common. Since the park is located west of the skyline, the later in the day you arrive, the better the light. This scene makes a wonderful panoramic, and it seems every time I've photographed this spot the clouds have been dramatic. Perhaps it has something to do with air from the cooler ocean nearby, meeting the heat generated from the city. The park also affords a view of the Statue of Liberty, although you are looking at her back and this is not her best angle. Liberty State Park offers convenient ferry departures to the Statue of Liberty itself.

Inside the city, magnificent views can be gained from the top of the Empire State Building as well as the top of Rockefeller Center. Hours vary for access to the two observation decks, but try for as early in the morning or as late in the day as possible. A classic view of the skyline can be seen from below the Brooklyn Bridge with the skyline behind. This is a particularly great night shot. Shooting west in the summer, post-sunset, and matching the glow from the sky with the city lights as it gets darker, is a classic shot. Brooklyn Bridge Park itself provides an excellent vantage point.

Tripods allowed, but likely not at Empire State Building or Rockefeller Center.

Nearby locations: The Statue of Liberty (mentioned above) resides on a small island, so photo possibilities are somewhat limited. The statue faces southeast and any kind of dramatic clouds or spot-lighting would be helpful. Otherwise, you may be able to join a helicopter tour from New York City, and using a long lens, capture the statue with Manhattan buildings beyond. The Statue of Liberty is struck by lighting frequently. So much so, that visiting during a thunderstorm might yield an amazing shot. Please make sure you are not a target, by the way. Firework displays happen several times a year here, and could contribute to a great image.

Cherry Blossoms – Washington, D.C.

The annual cherry blossom bloom among the monuments of America's Capitol is a brief but eye-dazzling spectacle. There are numerous opportunities to frame Washington's monuments with the almost 4,000 trees present around the Tidal Basin of the National Mall. The Jefferson Memorial is located on the Tidal Basin and works especially well with the trees. There are also individual groups of trees situated around the Washington Monument. Timing is everything and the event varies each year. The trees typically bloom over a two week period unless they are damaged by heavy wind or rain. April 4 is the average peak date, but that has varied from mid-March to mid-April over the years. If you really want to get the best images of this event, a little planning is essential.

My personal strategy was to stay with relatives in the area, and I worked some of the surrounding parks and scenic locales (Shenandoah National Park, Harpers Ferry, Chesapeake Bay), while waiting for peak bloom to occur. Another idea is to monitor the event on several websites that predict the peak period, and fly or drive to D.C. on short notice. These predictions are usually right, but not necessarily, and you may not be able to find lodging at the last minute. During the peak bloom, you will find parking difficult, and hordes of visitors. One way to circumvent both problems is to shoot very early in the morning. Arriving before dawn will probably allow you to find a parking spot. The reduced likelihood of wind at this time will also be helpful. Visiting on a weekday morning will limit the crowd factor even further. If no lodging is available close to Washington, consider staying in Maryland or Virginia. There are many hotels less than an hour away from the Capitol.

Cherry Blossoms & Jefferson Memorial

I suggest you apply for a permit to photograph on the Mall. After 9-11, rangers and park police are nervous about tripods (think missile launcher) and a permit will help you in every area except the White House and the Capitol. These are no-tripod zones unless you're from CNN. Apply for the permit ahead of time, and pick it up from the Mall NPS office, conveniently located near the Tidal Basin.

The Great Smoky Mountains – Tennessee & North Carolina

The Appalachian Mountains are beautiful throughout their many thousands of miles. As they come close to ending in the American South, the number of

plant species explodes and the mountains reach great heights. In the past, the warmer weather helped make life easier for the many settlers who came to live in this wilderness.

One of America's most visited parks, Great Smoky has amazing scenery and strong seasonal variety. Come in winter to avoid the

Hepatica & Spring Beauty

crowds and shoot fresh snow in the crystal-clear, frigid air. Travel to Newfound Gap in winter to photograph fog lapping against the peaks, or in spring, shoot the many successive mountain ridges stacked up in the distance from an overlook on Clingmans Dome Road. Also in spring, look for fields of trillium and other wildflowers in the forest near The Chimney Tops. Great waterfalls are everywhere, if the snow is melting or the rains are copious.

Autumn is my favorite time. If you come, book your campsite or hotel early. Autumn lasts a long time here, as it starts high on the mountain tops and cascades downward over several weeks. My all-time favorite fall shot is taken from the unpaved Rich Mountain Road above Cades Cove. At one pullout, you can see the tiny white historic Methodist Church below you, dwarfed by the mountains. In fall, the side-lighting here is fantastic, and the mountains are a sea of red as the sun descends. Many people come to capture this image, but they all leave too early. Stay until the fat lady sings! The church will have a tiny bit of light on its right side, but its white steeple and walls show up well in the shadows. Just as the sun is ready to disappear, the forest catches fire and it's time to shoot. The drive back to Townsend for lodging, food, and drink from there is a short one.

Cades Cove in Autumn, Great Smoky Mountains

Okefenokee Swamp at sunset

Swamps & Wetlands of the American South

The American South has a landscape to match its cultural significance. From William Faulkner to Robert Johnson to Elvis to Creedence and True Blood, the swamps of the South are evocative of mystery and danger, but also wilderness and unique beauty. And they happen to smell as good as anywhere on Earth.

Perhaps the most significant swamp is the Everglades in Florida. I have always found the "Glades" to be difficult to shoot, but Clyde Butcher has made a stellar career of photographing this area in black and white. I've had my best luck doing aerial shots of the Thousand Islands area and the great storms that attack the place. The Everglades doesn't have the big swamp tree you will find in Louisiana, Georgia and most of the other nearby states: the bald cypress.

This great tree—the bigger the better—comes in many shapes and sizes, and is usually covered in a drapery known as Spanish moss. For the best shots, hire a guide to take you to the big cypress areas of the Atchafalaya Swamp when the water is calm and a great sunrise or sunset is on the horizon. Add some morning fog, and all the elements of a great image are present. Bald cypress trees don't have leaves, but their needles turn a bright red in autumn, a great time to visit the area. One of the most photographed trees in the world is here—not a cypress but a live oak tree called the Evangeline Oak, in St. Martinville, Louisiana. Other great swamps include Reelfoot Lake in Tennessee, the huge Okefenokee Swamp in Georgia, Congaree Swamp National Park in South Carolina, and Merchants Millpond State Park in North Carolina.

Texas Wildflowers

When the winter rains have been prolific, and the timing is right, the Hill Country of Texas becomes a mass of wildflowers. During this fortunate time, huge fields of Texas bluebonnets and massive displays of Indian paintbrush bloom here, along with numerous other beautiful species. According to the popular song, Texas is the only place on Earth bluebonnets grow.

Wildflowers have become such a part of the culture here that Lady Bird Johnson founded a wildflower center near her Johnson City, Texas home. The keys to shooting Texas wildflowers are: arriving during a good year, arriving during peak bloom, and finding the best locations. All three factors can vary, but 2010 saw the biggest bloom in 50 years. The most prolific locations were along Highway 16, heading west and south of Dallas. Particular hotspots were in the vicinity of Willow City on the wildflower loop road there, and of course,

Texas bluebonnets & pholx

west of Austin in the LBJ park area. Several websites offer wildflower predictions and you can hear hotline information in season at 1-800-452-9292. Most Texas wildflowers are hardy and can hold their beauty for several weeks.

Wind is a common problem for flower photography on the Texas Plains. Morning is often a better time to avoid the stiff breezes, and using a higher ISO to stop motion is a good strategy. Sometimes, you just have to wait it out.

Carlsbad Caverns – New Mexico

Carlsbad Caverns is the most photographer-friendly major cave in the world. Many people think it is the most beautiful, as well. Photographers and tripods are allowed into all the areas of the cave visited by self-guided trails. On tours

Temple of the Sun

which take you to the major formations like the 'Christmas Tree' and the foreboding 'Klansman', the ranger has the option to allow tripods. Tripods are tolerated providing the group is small and your photo work does not hold up the tour. Small groups would be more likely in the off-season and you can still carry a camera along, even if tripods are not allowed in. Reservations for guided tours are required.

In the film days, the lights in the cave cast a troubling green color. Now with color temperature control in Lightroom and Photoshop, however, that problem can be mitigated. The 'Temple of the Sun' is perhaps one of the finest formations on the self-guided part of the tour, along with the 'Hall of Giants'. The park is accessible by car and open all year.

Other photogenic caves include the Skocjan Cave in Slovenia. Here you are able to view a huge underground river below and the opening used for the exit is like something out of Lord of the Rings. Though cameras are technically not allowed, people frequently take them in around their necks and shoot away like crazy. Visit this cave when humidity is low. When I was there, the amazing chamber with the river below was filled with fog. As you leave the cave, shoot the great waterfalls and arches.

Cliff Palace, Mesa Verde National Park – Colorado

On a high mesa in Western Colorado, the ancient structure that epitomizes the term cliff dwelling fills a large grotto in the canyon walls. Cliff Palace is big and beautiful and is well worth an investment of your time. Mesa Verde National Park is open all year, allowing a seasonal approach to photographing the brooding ruins. But since it faces southwest like most of the ruins in the American Southwest, direct light on the ruin is a winter phenomenon.

Photography may be possible on the ranger-led Cliff Palace tour, but at times tripods are not allowed, and tours are not usually undertaken in times of good lighting. My suggestion is to shoot Cliff Palace from overlooks that allow views of the ruin. The trail to the Palace Tour, before the locked gate, offers views down on the ruin from above. Be careful not to leave the trail here. Also, the ruin can be seen from the front at a viewpoint across the can-

Cliff Palace in winter

yon near the Sun Temple. During winter sunsets, both vantage points will provide beautiful lighting of the towers and rooms of this majestic dwelling. Since snow is common at Mesa Verde and it adds a feeling of mystery to the ruins and landscape, I've often shot there during winter. The roads are usually plowed

Far View Ruin at winter dawn

promptly, and if they're not, you can walk or ski on them out to the viewpoints (let a ranger know what you're up to). Of course, you'll need a good snow-worthy truck or SUV, just to get to the ranger station.

Nearby locations: Spruce Tree House is one of the most accessible of all the ruins. Next to the Visitor Center, the trail leading down to the structure is almost always open. A candelaria event there in December is a great photo opportunity. Another favorite ruin is Square Tower House, which provides great panoramic framing.

Spruce Tree House

The Dallas Divide & Telluride – Colorado

In landscape photography parlance, a "road-kill" is a shot that can be easily done from the road. Highway 62 across the Dallas Divide in the San Juan Mountains of Colorado provides one of America's best road-kill locations. Although there are ways to get closer to the mountains than the paved road, none really provide better shooting locations than the pull-offs.

The mountains face mainly north, so winter shots are very backlit here, making late spring and summer good for shooting at both sunrise and sunset. In June which is spring at this high elevation, the aspens turn an other-worldly green, while summer afternoons in July and August invariably bring rainbows and lightning. Good side-lighting coincides with the aspens turning gold during the last week of September into early October. The timing of this not-to-be-missed event can vary, however. Many photographers like to use the picturesque split rail fences along the road as foregrounds, but be careful as drivers on the highway will have their eyes on the scenery and not you. The Dallas Divide is also a prime area for panoramics.

Nearby Telluride, Colorado is perhaps the most scenic mountain town in the lower 48 states. Its calendar follows that of the Dallas Divide, and it's the

Log fence and mountain dandelion

Wilson Peak seen through Alta ghost town window

jumping-off spot for many great photography locations. Many of these are also road-kill, although a 4-wheel drive is helpful for some of the treks. Just outside Telluride to the east, Colorado's most beautiful waterfall, Bridal Veil Falls crashes hundreds of feet from the surrounding alpine plateau. The best view can be had from the jeep road that climbs up to Black Bear Road. In autumn, many red and yellow trees can be found to use as foreground along this road, and rainbows can me seen in the mists on summer afternoons. The big show at Telluride though, is the 14,000 foot peaks of the San Miguel Range on the south side of town. You'll recognize the mountains as symbols of Coors Beer. The range is probably most beautiful in September and October when it is dusted by fresh snow and framed by aspens. Views like this are available along the road to Rico. A short distance along the road, a 4-wheel drive road climbs to the ghost town of Alta. In one old building facade, a derelict window provides unparalleled framing of the San Miguel Range. Use HDR at sunrise and sunset to hold detail in the sun-capped peaks and the dark finely-textured wood around the window opening.

The Maroon Bells – Colorado

A symbol of the Colorado Rockies, the Maroon Bells, just outside of Aspen, Colorado, has to be the most photographed subject in the state. Fabled for fall aspen colors with fresh autumn snow on the peaks, the Bells are nonetheless challenging to photograph.

Right: Maroon Bells reflection at sunrise

Like Mesa Arch in Utah, sometimes many photographers vie for prime locations on the shore of Maroon Lake. The Maroon Bells face northeast, and get the best frontal lighting in summer at dawn, but they get enough good sidelight through October for autumn shooting, as well. In winter and spring, the access road to Maroon Lakes and the view of the Maroon Bells is closed due to snow. Skiers and snowmobilers can use the road to visit the site, and although photographing in winter could be spectacular, the mountains will be quite backlit through most of the day. Spring trips by ski would provide lots of snow and better lighting. From the middle of June to Labor Day and on weekends in September the area is closed to car travel from 9am to 5pm. Since most photographers travel outside these hours, car travel is an option then. Many shooters hope for a calm lake surface, which is most likely in the morning. Remember that water reflections in shaded areas are superior to those where sunlight is hitting the surface and degrading the reflection. Sometimes, if the lake is too rough, small beaver ponds near the lake's outlet provide calm water for good reflections.

Mt. Rushmore – South Dakota

The Black Hills of South Dakota, rich in both history and scenic beauty, rise above the Great Plains and are harbingers of the Rocky Mountains farther west. The faces of four American presidents, carved in the granite face of Mount

Morning summer clouds over Mt. Rushmore

Rushmore, face southeast to greet the rising winter sun. Most people see and photograph the solemn visages in summer when the faces are evenly lit through the midday hours. Photographers who visit in winter will have better light, fewer crowds and the chance of snow on the pine forest that surrounds the viewing area. No one is allowed to venture anywhere in the Memorial except from the parking lot to the main viewing area, so there is only one primary vantage point. Also, stormy or uneven light has never seemed to work for me at Rushmore.

Aerial view of Mt. Rushmore at dawn

These are people's faces, after all, and they are people most Americans admire greatly, so I approach them with reverence.

One great way to capture a different view of the monument is from an airplane at dawn in the fall or winter months. The true setting for the sculptures is best seen this way, with Mount Rushmore rising above the trees and ridges of the granite domes of the Black Hills National Forest.

Tripods are sometimes not allowed, post 9-11.

Nearby locations: The number of great photo subjects in the Black Hills area is sizeable. Badlands National Park is a photographer's dream. Photogenic all year, it is very hot and humid in summer, while notoriously cold in winter. My favorite Badlands viewpoint is Sheep Mountain Table, which is great in summer, but requires a high-clearance vehicle to reach. America's first national monument, Devils Tower, is known by any moviegoer, and is in the Wyoming section of the Black Hills. For morning shots, try shooting the Tower with reflections from the Belle Fourche River. Late in the day, there are many vantage points to the west of the Tower, and it would make a great night shot.

Brink of Lower Falls & Yellowstone Canyon

Yellowstone National Park – Wyoming

Generally considered the world's first national park, Yellowstone has a huge array of subjects. It is one of the few places in this book having photographic guidebooks dedicated to one park alone. My attempt here will be to suggest the very best landscape opportunities at Yellowstone.

Grand Prismatic Spring takes the prize for the most colorful feature of the park. The largest hot spring in the world, Grand Prismatic's rainbow colors are a result of algae living at varying temperatures within the spring. This can't be seen well at ground level, but by climbing a small hill next to the spring, you'll have a great view. This is a midday sunny shot. You will need the sun overhead to bring out all the amazing color. An even better approach is to rent a small plane from West Yellowstone, Jackson, or Bozeman to shoot the spring from above.

Yellowstone Canyon, for which the park is named, is next on my list.

Right: Grand Prismatic Spring

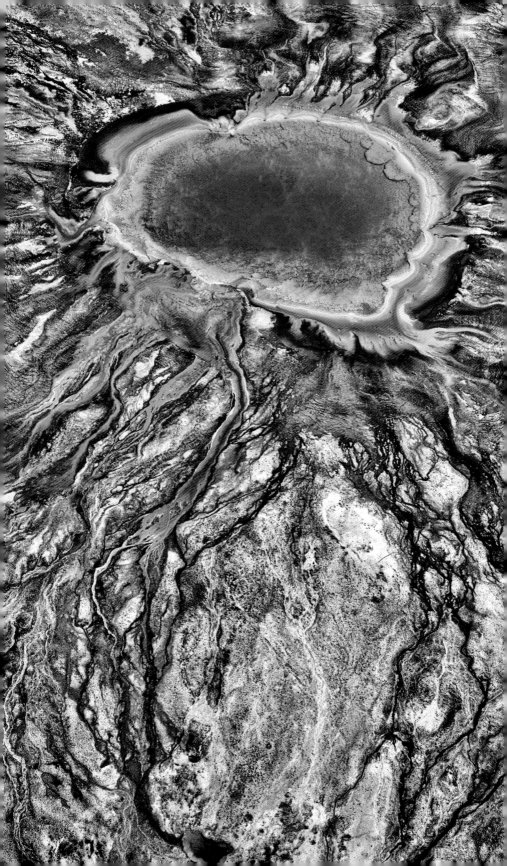

Great Fountain Geyser

The classic shot including the falls at Artist Point is best done as a summer sunrise using HDR, or as a midday shot while sunlight enhances the colors of the yellow canyon. For something different, try the trail that takes you to the lip of the Lower Falls and use a wide angle lens to include the canyon beyond. Leftover snow, which you might find when the park reopens in spring, adds a great additional element. Since it can snow anytime of year in Yellowstone, be prepared to use the white stuff as 'icing on the cake'. Other subjects include Great Fountain Geyser, a terraced reflecting pond. This subject works well at sunset in summer. Morning Glory Pool and Beauty Pools are very colorful, and Artemisia Pool with its deep blues and lacework travertine, is also good. I love Mammoth Hot Springs with its interesting formations, and it's the only part of the park that can be reached by car in winter. This mountain-like hot spring faces generally east, making it a good morning subject.

Traveling off-season in Yellowstone, if you are prepared, can be very productive. As mentioned, snowstorms can occur before park roads close in fall and after they re-open in the spring. Some wet snow on the trees around one of the great cascades like Tower Falls would add considerable interest. Winter in

Yellowstone is a different world and it's my favorite time to shoot geysers, since the steam from the eruptions meeting the cold air can easily double their apparent size. Rime ice covers many surfaces, and "ghost trees" covered in multiple layers of thick snow and ice are everywhere. Waterfalls emanating from warm geyser basins don't freeze and continue to run through the deep winter landscape.

Grand Teton National Park – Wyoming

This park, contiguous with Yellowstone, is famed for its dramatic spiky mountains, beautiful wildflower displays, and glistening lakes and rivers. Part of the Rocky Mountains, the peaks rise precipitously, sans foothills, from the Jackson Hole area. The most famous photography viewpoint is called Schwabacher's Landing. I was fortunate to be one of the first photographers to capture this scene in the 1970's.

Grand Teton rising above the clouds at sunset

Bradley Lake

Simply follow the signs on the good dirt road off highway 191 to the Snake River area, where you will find small beaver ponds to reflect the precipitous peaks at sunrise. Scouting the location the previous day would be helpful to find the beaver ponds and pick out a good spot. The river is constantly changing, so you may have to walk around to find the optimal vantage point. In the morning, I recommend you get up early as there will almost always be a crowd at the viewpoint. For other great reflections on calm mornings with smaller crowds, try Jenny and String Lakes and the Blacktail Ponds. Ansel Adams made the first noteworthy photographs at the Snake River Overlook, which is right off the highway. This spot is several hundred feet above the river with mountains as background. Ansel's most famous scene was backlit and featured dramatic clouds.

As for wildflowers, mule's ear flowers abound around the park in early June, and large fields of lupine can be found in numerous locations later in the month. Fall color comes early to the high country of the Tetons, and leaves can change as early as the second week in September. Just past Moran Junction, nice stands of aspens can be very appealing if the mountain peaks beyond have fresh snow. Finally, the Mormon Row barns (turn east just past Moose) are a great photo subject. With these amazing century-old barns below the looming peaks, you can't go wrong. As with most subjects in the park, sunrise and morning are the best. Spring is the time to shoot the snow-laden mountains with the barns and the green fields included.

Delicate Arch, Arches National Park – Utah

Though it's not the largest, or the most difficult to get to, Delicate Arch is probably the world's most famous natural arch. A free-standing structure at the top of a huge sandstone bowl, the arch is revealed suddenly at the end of a 1.5 mile hike with an elevation gain of several hundred feet.

Delicate Arch and I go back a long time. When I first started shooting the Arch, I would often be the only person there, even in spring, summer, and fall.

Right: Delicate Arch

Moonrise at Delicate Arch

It was at Delicate Arch I learned about the huge difference the sun's angle makes on the lighting of a landscape subject. In winter, the sun's light comes at a strong right angle to the bowl at sunset, lighting it beautifully. The arch itself, however, is not fully lit. In summer, the rocks behind the bowl place the foreground in shadow early in the sunset cycle, but the arch itself is fully lit with no shadows.

For years, I went to the arch hoping to capture a rainbow in the scene and finally succeeded some years ago. The best time for a rainbow is during summer thunderstorms, but the rainbow is frequently too far south to work well – the equinoxes are better for that. If you would like the distant La Sal Mountains in the background to have snow, November to May is best. Most images you've seen with a moon inside the Arch are double exposures. To get a real full moon shot, you need to be there in June on the night before the full moon—and this must occur close to the summer solstice. Even then, getting far enough west on the bowl for the shot is somewhat dangerous. Half and three-quarter moons can be shot with the arch throughout the year, all around the bowl area. I have been able to get rainbows, moons, reflections, heavy snow, and magnificent light at Delicate Arch, but my last goal is to get some good lightning: a dangerous, "don't try this at home" idea.

The viewing/shooting area at the arch is not huge, and many times there are hundreds of people in attendance for sunset. Though there have not been a large number of accidents there, the terrain is very steep, and should be approached with utmost caution. A common problem is people standing in the arch when you want to capture a sunset shot. All I can say is that they have as much right to be there as photographers do, and the best idea is to calmly ask them to move for a second. But if you can't beat them, why not join them. Getting up close to the arch can be really great with a wide angle or fisheye lens.

Mesa Arch, Canyonlands National Park – Utah

In the last decade, Mesa Arch has become the most-photographed location in the Moab, Utah area. Most photographers know the drill: arrive pre-dawn, walk the short distance to the arch and negotiate (peacefully, I hope) with the other photographers for a tripod position. The star of the show is the red glow on the underside of the arch at sunrise.

Before night photography became so popular, most photographers could be assured a spot here by getting up early and being the first to arrive. With many people spending the whole night there now—probably against park rules—it's hard to be first. I have many shots of Mesa Arch, so my only trips there in recent years have been with workshops. Adding a dozen people to the mix is always interesting. It's still the best idea to get there as soon as you can, whatever time of year you pick. You would think the Arch would see less visitation in summer than in winter, but this in not consistently the case. This could be because winter, early spring and late fall assure the sun will rise south of the La Sal Mountains and provide a lower, more intense red glow to the arch. The glow, by the way, comes from sunlight hitting the cliff below the arch and bouncing up on the already orange-colored Navajo sandstone. If you arrive in May, the sun must take an additional five minutes when the light is warmest, to clear the distant

Mesa Arch at dawn

mountains. You will want to shoot the glow without lens flare. This means secur-
ing a shooting angle so that the arch can block the sun. It takes the sun about
twenty minutes, depending on the time of year, to rise above the arch. At that
point, the glow fades, the show's over and everyone leaves.

If you want an image of the whole arch, a focal length of 16mm or smaller is
necessary. To emphasize the glow and the pinnacles in the canyon, try including just part of the arch with a longer lens. Due to the extreme depth-of-field
required for this shot, focus stacking software could be employed post-capture,
to make everything sharp. There are actually many compositions at Mesa Arch,
especially if you have some clouds to go along with the glowing arch. Shooting
from above, for instance, with a telephoto lens can make a unique image.

Monument Valley – Arizona & Utah

I've spent a great deal of time shooting Monument Valley, and enjoyed
every minute. The photographer who popularized this dramatic location, Josef
Muench, supposedly visited
the Valley 700 times. I don't
think that's too many. It's
obviously been photographed
a lot, so if you get something
unique, you're fortunate.

A normal entrance pass
allows you to drive around
the tourist loop road to shoot
in the main valley and at the
Mittens overlook. The primi-
tive camping area to the north
of the main parking lot is
also included. To get there,
proceed down the valley drive
and continue north for a short
distance to a large dirt parking
area.

The Totem Pole & Yei Bi Chei rocks

No hiking is allowed with
the Valley Drive pass, but with good light some decent images can be acquired
along the route. If time permits, take it to the next level and join a sunrise
or sunset tour or hire your own personal Navajo guide. Doing this will allow
you to visit and shoot the Totem Pole (best at dawn) and the dunes, beautiful all year long, but especially great at dawn looking north toward the big
monuments. Another excellent spot outside the main valley is Teardrop
Arch, which frames the Utah Monuments beautifully at sunset from April

Right: The Totem Pole & the Milky Way

The Totem Pole at sunset

to August. The trip to teardrop is short compared to the more distant valley locations. Many other arches can be seen in the main valley and in Mystery Valley, another guided location. To kick it up yet another notch, join a tour to Hunt's Mesa, an adventurous overnight off-road trip to a high mesa looking northward across the whole valley. This trip is best done near the equinoxes when side-lighting is optimal. The view here escapes verbal description.

In winter, snow may fall on the dunes and produce fascinating patterns as they melt. Also, fog can be a common condition in the valley at this time of year, adding to the mystery of this singular landscape. In summer, thunderstorms are accompanied by amazing clouds, lightning, and rainbows. With no electric lights in the valley and no cities within a hundred miles or more, Monument Valley is a wonderland for night photography. At this time, the only way to do this is to join a Monument Valley by Night Tour from Moab Photo Tours.

Horseshoe Bend Overlook, Glen Canyon – Arizona

One of the many scenic wonders around Page, Arizona, the Horseshoe Bend Overlook on the Colorado River before it enters Grand Canyon, is perhaps the best river vista in the world! A short distance south of Page, a sign guides visitors to an easy walk to the canyon's edge, one thousand feet above an amazing u-turn in the river's course.

The shot is a sunrise/early morning affair, with sun making its way all the way down into the canyon fairly quickly during summer months. A wide angle lens and some bravery help get the entire bend in view. The river, which has just passed through the Glen Canyon Dam upstream, is often a striking blue or green color. Late day or sunset shots might be possible in HDR, and I have tried for years to capture the bend in snow, which is an extremely rare occurrence.

Other rivers in the Southwest with photogenic bends include the Goosenecks of the San Juan River near Mexican Hat, Utah. With a stitched panoramic image, it's possible to get four giant bends of the river in one shot. The goosenecks are best shot at midday. The Gooseneck of the Colorado River is the main attraction of Dead Horse Point State Park, near Moab, Utah. This Gooseneck can be approached more closely on a dirt road leading south from Highway 279 past the Moab Salt Plant. Shooting at dawn with a wide angle lens is recommended.

Horseshoe Bend of the Colorado River

Antelope Canyon – Arizona

In the late 1970's, I noticed a strange notation on a map of Lake Powell. Near the lake and the town of Page, Arizona, a canyon was labeled "Corkscrew Canyon." Always curious about the names of physical features, I made plans to visit. I left the adjacent highway and drove up Antelope Canyon, a sandy, nonde-

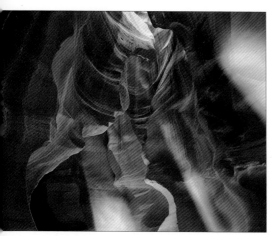

Antelope Canyon light rays

script desert wash, being the supposed location of the "Corkscrew". After a few miles, I could go no further. The wash ended at a rock wall, with a surprisingly thin opening that cleaved the rock in two. As I entered on foot, I realized that I was seeing something incredibly special, and photographically unparalleled.

Sunlight entering the top of the canyon cascaded down through a small slit from above and bounced like a supercharged billiard ball around the narrow sculpted walls below. The colors were unlike anything else I had seen in nature: reds, violets, pinks, oranges, yellows, and even blues moved around the undulating walls rapidly as the sun angle changed the scene minute-by-minute. The walls glowed with an inner neon luminosity unlike anything I had ever observed. I was not the first photographer to shoot in Upper Antelope Canyon, but I was certainly among the first.

Using a 4x5 camera and determining how to shoot in a totally alien setting was a challenge for me. My exposures were often several minutes long, and I had to be careful about "hot spots" of direct light that would almost burn a hole in the film. I entered the canyon once on a windy day and noticed "sandfalls" blowing into the canyon that created shafts of heavenly light. I believe I was the first pho-tographer to discover this, and I was fortunate to have images of it published in Arizona Magazine, at the time. Sometime later, my friends who were good with ropes, helped me get into Lower Antelope Canyon, which was also magnificent. I remember thinking at the time that these two canyons were so special, I hoped the Navajos would find a way to protect them. For mostly economic reasons, this has happened, and now on most mornings hundreds of photographers and regular tourist buses arrive at Upper Antelope Canyon.

At times, photography is difficult because of the number of people in the canyon, but it is certainly easier with digital equipment. There are a few tricks to photographing in these canyons, as I will elaborate. The best lighting effects come from about April 1 to September 1, and mid-day is usually best.

Right: Light ray entering Antelope Canyon

Images taken in winter tend to be much more drab, but have more blues than those shot during the peak seasons. Undesired hot spots, places where shafts of light directly hit the canyon floor or walls, can now be removed digitally. Photographers here often work together to throw sand in the air, mimicking my wind effect. Lower Antelope Canyon does not have quite the crowds that visit the upper canyon, and in many ways is just as beautiful.

The Wave, Paria/Vermillion Cliffs Wilderness

The Coyote Buttes & the 'Wave' – Arizona

I would not have included this fragile site in Northern Arizona if the number of people visiting was not controlled. I made a recent visit to the site and thankfully, could not see any major degradation of the Wave's beauty since I first visited there in the 1980's. Others I have talked to think they see some strong evidence of damage. At any rate, walking around the wave itself, not bringing dogs, and going barefoot will help cut down on this erosion. The Wave itself, a fairly small area of amazing sculpted sandstone reminiscent of an ocean wave, has become justifiably world-famous among photographers. It probably tops the list of American desert wonders for many people. No one who visits this sandstone masterpiece comes away disappointed.

A permit is required to hike the three miles into the Wave in North Coyote Buttes, and at times they are nearly impossible to acquire. The number of people hoping to visit the Wave, especially in pleasant spring and fall temperatures, exceeds the number allowed, often considerably. To apply for a permit, which is awarded by lottery, visit the BLM's website at: www.blm.gov/az/st/en/arolrsmain/paria/coyote_buttes.html

The Wave is not really a sunrise or sunset shot, although it does work tolerably well with HDR or GND assistance. Shooting the Wave in overcast conditions doesn't work well either. My favorite time to go is in November or late January, when sunlight enters the Wave area for only about 90 minutes. This is a time when fewer people visit Coyote Buttes due to cold and inclement weather, so getting a permit is less difficult. From the standard viewpoint—the best one in my opinion— above the Wave, the low sun illuminates the Wave from behind you and emphasizes the striations that give the wave its character. You will be shooting toward the north. When the sun does finally fill the bowl, you will have to move into a position to crop out your own shadow, which can easily be done. You will then have an hour or more to work before a distracting shadow encroaches from the left.

Tread softly on this precious place, and pay attention to your route in and out, as becoming lost is a common problem.

Bryce Canyon National Park – Utah

World-renowned for its collection of colorful spires and hoodoos, Bryce Canyon is perhaps unequaled in the world for erosional complexity. Though the park is large, the best examples of erosion are mostly in one small area: Bryce Amphitheater. And, though Bryce has lookouts titled Sunrise Point and Sunset Point, it is almost completely a sunrise location for photographers.

Since the Amphitheater is a curved bowl about three miles in size facing east, there is almost always a place to use the sunrise along the rim. At sunset, especially in winter, the bowl fills with shadows quickly, making photography of the pinnacle-filled landscape challenging. At 8,000 feet, Bryce Canyon is a storm magnet, making it a great place to work with copious winter snow and frequent violent (but beautiful) thunderstorms. As the sun ascends on the horizon, an amazing feature of Bryce Canyon becomes noticeable. The light from the formations bounces around, creating reflected light on surrounding hoodoos.

Spring Snow in morning light

I have seen effects like this in several other locations, but I think it is most common and easiest to photograph at Bryce.

Besides shooting from the rim, Bryce offers many great shooting opportunities on its interior trails. These include astounding trees reaching for the sun from deep in the canyons, small natural arches, eroded sandstone fantasies and bristlecone pine trees, one of the world's oldest living things. In winter, due to heavy snowfall, only the roads around the Amphitheater are kept open. In summer, the road continues many miles beyond the Amphitheater before ending at Yovimpa Point. My favorite spots along this road include the Natural Bridge, Rainbow Point (with a great sunset shot of The Hunter), and Fairyland Canyon, right at the park's entry boundary. Fairyland has a large number of deep red-orange pinnacles that glow with reflected light in summer.

Remember, you will be typically shooting east into the sun at Bryce Canyon and will need to protect your lens with a shade or your hand. Helicopter trips are also an option here; those leaving early in the morning work best.

Winter Sunrise at Bryce

Sunrise on Zion peaks

The Towers of the Virgin, Zion National Park – Utah

The viewpoint for the Towers of the Virgin works well almost all year for sunrise and is very easy to get to. To visit this site, locate the old visitor center—west of the highway that runs from Springdale to Zion Canyon. The facility is now an office complex, with lots of parking. This is a sunrise shot only that works best in winter, but will work acceptably all year.

Since the huge sandstone peaks you are shooting are so high, they receive a lot of snow in winter, and they are at their most beautiful during a clearing snowstorm with sunlight on the peaks. After parking near the old headquarters, walk around the right hand side of the building to the back where you will see a picnic table and a sign naming the spires. You will shoot from here. There is usually a small crowd on hand at dawn, but since there is plenty of room, this won't be an issue. Wait for the light, and hope for something spectacular. A panoramic when the first line of light appears is a great option.

Nearby location: The classic image of the Watchman at sunset taken from the bridge over the Virgin River almost made the 'A' list for this book. The river itself makes great foreground and clouds really help this composition. In early to mid-November the cottonwoods along the river turn deep yellow and make this shot sing!

The 'Subway', Zion National Park – Utah

In a land of beautiful canyons, the 'Subway'—a very unique canyon in Zion National Park—may be at the top of the list. In that regard, it's to my knowledge the only canyon in the state that controls the number of visitors each day. I'm fairly certain that I was the first photographer with a 4x5 camera to visit the Subway and publish photographs of it. This was in a time when there were no trails, and no guidebook telling me what to expect. I made many more trips, including one from the very top, through the so-called Upper Subway. I made another hike at autumn's end, probably ill-advised, when the creek was overflowing its banks and the Subway itself was covered in snow.

If you succeed in getting a permit, make sure your camera is in a waterproof pack. Be ready for a fairly long hike up and down the lava wall, and up to the 'Subway' and back with multiple stream crossings. The canyon is full of lava rocks that have a deserved reputation for being slippery. Take extra care here as you are far from medical help.

After several hours of hiking, your first clue that the 'Subway' is near are the stairstep Archangel Cascades. Photos of this unusual tiered waterfall with fall color are some of my most popular stock and gallery images. Try not to be at this spot during midday when the sun is high overhead. You want even lighting from canyon wall shadows or clouds for the rest of your trip. If a sunny day is forecast, that's fine, just get a very early start or begin after lunch. More waterfalls continue right up to the Subway keyhole, a slot canyon with a narrow top and a round chamber below. Several large clear pools make a great foreground. Return the way you came, making sure you have time to climb the wall out with some sunlight in the sky.

The Grand Canyon – Arizona

The Grand Canyon in Grand Canyon National Park is a true scenic wonder of the world. Anyone who comes into its orbit has no soul if they are not mesmerized, stunned, amazed or instantly in love. For photographers, the gift is the world's greatest landscape combined with some of the world's greatest light. But the challenge is how to shrink all this majesty into a two-dimensional image.

Fortunately the canyon helps us. The rims survey huge areas of land where light is almost always falling somewhere. From the South Rim, the sun's angle is perfect for many viewpoints throughout the year, with especially good side-lighting around the equinoxes. Sunrises can be quite good as the sun rises over the lower, less cloudy Painted Desert region to the east. Work quick, as lighting can change very rapidly here.

Weather will also be your friend at Grand Canyon, unless you arrive on a winter's day when clouds and mists can obscure everything. In moderation, the fog can create wonderful moods. Summer thunderstorms, especially in July, August,

Left: The Subway's waterfalls and pools in summer afternoon light

Evening clouds at Mather Point

and September create storm light, great clouds, lightning, and rainbows. In winter, the high elevation brings snow—sometimes just a dusting, other times many inches. My strategy is to watch for the prediction of stormy weather, get in place at the canyon before it hits, and work the bad weather through to conclusion. The dying throes of a storm are always the best.

The best 'all-purpose' South Rim viewpoint is Mather Point. You can drive there easily and the view from Mather up and down the canyon is considerable. Other favorites are Lipan, Grandview, Desert View, and Moran points on the East Rim Drive. Hopi and Maricopa Points on the West Rim are good also but must be reached by a free park bus.

The North Rim of the Canyon, only open from about May to November, is higher, cooler, and has fewer viewpoints. Cape Royal is a great site, with views in all directions. On the North Rim, you are much closer to the huge inner-canyon buttes that give the place so much of its splendor. These places do not allow as much freedom to follow the light, so with only a few visits, luck will have to be with you. I have spent a lot of time on the North Rim and only have a small number of quality images to show for it. The place is so spectacular in summer, however, that setting up camp and waiting for a great scene can be utter bliss.

After a long drive over sometimes impassable roads, Toroweap, one of the North Rim's lower viewpoints, is a great view. Photographically, however, all the low-hanging fruit has been taken, and achieving an unusual shot there would be difficult. Capturing a new look with HDR might prove appealing, and I'll be trying that approach soon. The attraction at Toroweap is a 3,000 foot cliff dropping straight down to the Colorado River. There is a lot of good foreground material, and the view upstream is the classic one, captured at either sunrise or sunset.

Cape Royal at dusk

Viewing the canyon from the river is one of the best backcountry trips in the world, and though expensive, outfitters provide a very easy way for you and your camera to get into places of overpowering beauty. Besides the big vistas, you can see and photograph the river and its reflections, ancient Puebloan ruins, slot canyons and beautiful grottoes filled with water. Several waterfalls come right off the cliffs into the river. Furthermore, you will be in camp during the magic hours of sunrise and sunset, free to exploit the great light of those periods.

Marble Canyon

Poppy field in California's high desert

Antelope Valley Poppy Reserve – California

Though far from a sure thing, the California Poppy Reserve in the high desert near Los Angeles is a tremendous sight and a wonderful photographic opportunity. The small reserve, surrounded by desert mountains and encroaching cities, preserves a small patch of what must have been an ocean of floral color as far and the eye could see.

Spring, when the flowers bloom, is of course the windiest time of the year. This adds to the challenge of being in place in a good year, and trying to shoot as close to the peak of bloom as possible. Further, the poppy blossoms close up in late afternoon and don't open again until morning. Besides the poppies, you may find owl's clover, goldfields, and perhaps even lupine for a larger color palette. Rains in the fall, winter and early spring are needed for the best displays. In 2008, the bloom was especially good, while several years earlier the bloom was truly spectacular all over Southern California, including Death Valley National Park and Carrizo Plain National Monument. Carrizo Plain, a newer park, was covered with flowers in a psychedelic blaze of color. The Poppy Preserve web site gives timely and accurate information about the bloom prognosis throughout the year.

California's Big Trees

It's amazing to think that the world's largest, tallest, and oldest trees are all found in California. The coastal Redwoods, the tallest of which are almost 400 feet high, are truly a challenge to your photographic skills, due to their enormity. Lying on your back using an extreme wide angle lens is one solution. Another

Waterfalls cascading through Sequoias in Spring snowmelt

Eastern Sierra Nevada range reflection in Owens Lake

option is to visit the trees in the morning, when sunbeams illuminated by fog create beautiful darts of light. Rhododendrons typically bloom in May here and provide a splash of color to the scene.

At Sequoia National Park, the trees are also a challenge. They are not as tall as the Redwoods, but much heftier. The road to the park is kept open all winter, and visiting the big trees with a new dusting of snow and the sun peaking out after a storm is euphoric. Also, when the snow melts in June after a heavy winter, large streams of snowmelt run through the trees.

In the White Mountains of the Inyo National Forest, south of Sequoia, the Bristlecone Pine Forest features some of the world's oldest living things, including trees that are 4,700 years old. Though bristlecones grow throughout the entire range, the Schulman and Patriarch Groves are the best places to go at sunrise or sunset. Since the whole Eastern Sierra is a place of high mountains and deep valleys, dramatically shaped lenticular clouds (often appearing like 'flying saucers') are common, making great additions to your tree images. The bristlecones themselves are perfect subjects for 'intimate landscapes' and the weathered and twisted structure of each tree is unique. Their bodies and limbs are a symphony of pattern and texture.

Bristlecone pine trees are fascinating photo subjects and can be found in California, Nevada, Arizona, Utah and Colorado. Places to find these trees are the Great Basin National Park, Bryce Canyon National Park, Cedar Breaks National Monument and Dixie National Forest. A favorite location of mine is in Ashdown Gorge Wilderness near the Utah ski town of Brian Head called the Twisted Forest. You won't find much information about this site, so you'll have to get directions locally.

Eastern Sierra Nevada & Owens Valley – California

Few areas in America can boast the number and quality of photo locations as the lee, or eastern side, of the great Sierra Nevada Mountain Range. The east-facing half of the range is almost a desert because the western Sierras scrape the clouds from the nearby Pacific nearly dry as they pass. Water is still part of the scene here, however, along with amazing rock formations, ghost towns, rock art, natural arches, bristlecone pines and cloud formations deformed by the high peaks.

Two of America's greatest landscape photographers concentrated extensively on this relatively small area: Ansel Adams and Galen Rowell. Seen in countless movies even up to the present day (Gladiator and Iron Man included), the Alabama Hills are so beautiful and alien, they can stand in for desert Europe or the Middle East.

Alabama Hills Arch in Owens Valley

Besides the rocks themselves, the area is home to dozens of natural arches, many of which neatly frame mountains rising two miles above the valley.

If you make your base in Lone Pine, you will have easy access to the Alabama Hills and the nearby Owens Lake. If the lake is full, and you stop along Highway 136, a few miles south of town, you can get a magnificent panoramic reflection of the entire Southern Sierra in its brackish waters. With a good four wheel drive in the summer months, you can visit the privately-owned ghost town of Cerro Gordo. Elsewhere, in the White Mountains, you'll find examples of some of the world's oldest and eminently photographable trees, the bristlecone pines. Again, this area is a summer-only location, high in the range.

BLM offices in Lone Pine and Bishop provide maps to nearby rock art panels, some of which can be photographed with the mountains looming in the background. The season you choose to visit is important. In winter and spring, the mountains are usually anointed with snow, and it's relatively warm in the valley. In summer, the high terrain is accessible and cool, while the valley is hot.

Yosemite National Park – California

In addition to being a scenic mecca for the whole world, Yosemite National Park claims many distinctions. The birthplace of the environmental movement,

Yosemite Falls reflection

the location where the science of glaciers was formulated and the home of the world's best known landscape photographer are among them. Many books have been written about how to photograph Yosemite, so I will hit only the highlights here.

Yosemite is a fairly low valley in the midst of the highest mountain range in the lower 48 United States. It is carved like much of the Sierra Nevada range, from beautiful light-colored granite. Yosemite Valley is just one segment of the park. When summer arrives, access is available to higher elevations which offer viewpoints of the Valley and photogenic mountains and meadows. The Valley is lush in spring and summer and is famous for views of Half Dome, El Capitan, Yosemite Falls, and more. A reflecting pond on the Merced River is a favorite for photographers when the river is low in fall and winter. The pond works best at sunset and is located just downstream from El Capitan on the north side of the Valley, near Valley View. The great waterfalls like Yosemite (one of the highest in the world) and Bridalveil are at their best during the winter and spring, after Sierra snows melt. In spring especially, there are many ponds reflecting the Valley's features and waterfalls. Please stay on trails and boardwalks and don't give photographers a bad name by slogging through pristine marshlands to get a shot.

El Capitan & Yosemite walls reflected in Merced River

As summer approaches, crowds swell, but access to the upper Merced River waterfalls, Nevada and Vernal opens up. Vernal has a nice rainbow in the morning from viewpoints along the trail. With Tioga Pass and the Glacier Point Road open in summer, there are many opportunities to shoot looking into the valley from high above. Glacier Point itself provides a northerly view which is perfect for both sunrise and sunset.

Many of the great Ansel Adams images were made in winter, and with few people in the park, this is a great time to visit. Yosemite Falls faces almost directly south, so light is best on the falls during the winter and on summer mornings. One of Ansel Adam's signature shots of the valley was taken after a snowstorm from Valley View, which is west of the valley and a great sunset location. During a wet year, you can count on a good snowstorm if you spend a week. With a dry, warm winter, there may be no snow falling in the valley at all. Horsetail Falls, first photographed by Galen Rowell, sometimes runs during the winter, and in the last two weeks of February catches the low sunlight from behind and looks like it's on fire.

Bodie Ghost Town at sunset

Bodie Ghost Town – California

Bodie is easily the best ghost town in the United States, and an amazing relic of the Wild West. The size of the town and the large numbers of decaying buildings is unmatched. Also unmatched are the range of images that can be made here, from close-ups to grand scenics.

The only thing missing at Bodie is a stunning backdrop, since the view of Bodie does not include the Sierra Nevada range nearby. At over 8,000 feet elevation, however, Bodie gets some wonderful clouds, as well as snow and rain storms. A dusting of snow really adds to the ambience of the deserted town. The Methodist Church is my personal favorite. Unfortunately, the town is not open during "magic hour" except during October, when the 8 AM opening may closely match sunrise toward the end of the month. I have also shot wide images of the whole town (panoramics work well here) from the parking lot, after the gates are closed and the light is good. Sometimes the park runs photography tours at night, and allows shooting inside buildings not normally open to the public.

North America has dozens of photo-ready ghost towns throughout the West. Kennecott Ghost Town in Wrangell/St. Elias National Park and Preserve in Alaska, America's largest national park, is one of the best. The town is easy to get to and is situated below huge glacier-clad peaks for added drama. You can fly from Anchorage to the town of McCarthy and stay just outside the park. The beautiful Root Glacier is also there.

The Fly Geyser – Nevada

Although man-made, Fly Geyser is a continuously erupting, very colorful feature unlike just about anything in the world! It is located on the edge of the huge Black Rock Desert north of Reno, Nevada. Sunrise or sunset, it really doesn't matter; the geyser is always going and always beautiful.

Located on private land, the geyser is currently off-limits to photographers unless they pay $1,000 and post a bond to cover any destruction to the geyser. When I originally wrote this entry, the news was better. The owners had proposed a full-time recreational resort and campground on the land where the geyser is located. This was great news, first, since there's no good place to stay in the area, and second, it seemed access to the geyser for photographers would be assured. Only time will tell if this proposal will become reality, but for now you'll be trespassing if you visit without permission.

I've noticed in comparing my images of the geyser taken about ten years ago that the newer images have much more green. It also looks like people are using small ladders to get a higher angle. This sounds smart but could be very dangerous to both the photographer and the geyser.

The Fly Geyser, Black Rock Desert

A permit from the site's private owners is required and tripods are allowed with the permit.

Other photogenic geysers in the American West include those in Yellowstone National Park (more under its own entry) and the Green River Geyser near the town of Green River, Utah, one of the overlooked wonders of the West. A non-natural geyser like Fly, it is powered by CO_2, and emits cold water on an irregular schedule. The eruptions send hundreds of gallons of water over a series of orange travertine dams into the river. The whole area is exposed to the setting sun year-round, and if you could time the eruption with sunset, it could provide some great images. Directions to the geyser and estimates of its next eruption can be obtained at the Powell River Museum in Green River. It is a short drive from the town to this drive-in location.

San Francisco's Golden Gate Bridge

The Golden Gate Bridge – California

The Golden Gate Bridge is reputed to be the most photographed bridge in the world. Fortunately, the National Park Service has created several viewpoints on the north side of the bridge, including some new lookouts that are positioned relatively high above the structure. These allow great views of the city, beyond the world-famous span. Further, the scenic parking areas may allow you to get high enough to get great photos of the bridge rising above fog, very common during summer months. This view of the bridge from the high viewpoints is a sunset shot, with light from the west illuminating the whole bridge, the water and downtown San Francisco. It could work well in the morning too, when the fog is most likely to be present.

Heceta Head Lighthouse

Heceta Head Lighthouse – Oregon

Generally considered the most beautiful lighthouse on the Western U.S. Coast, and in the most beautiful setting, Heceta Head Lighthouse is in the perfect position to pick up a great side-lit sunset. The distant forested headlands add to the scene and waves from March to May and from July to September provide further embellishment.

Winter months will bring backlighting for this subject, but with a long lens there is a shot from the road south of the lighthouse that works on winter afternoons. Getting the sun to appear from behind the clouds spawned by the ocean is the trick. I made seven trips to this location to get the last glow of sun peaking

out from underneath the drizzly clouds. An ultrawide angle lens (14-18mm) is a must here. The hike to the lighthouse is fairly short, and weekdays during the early spring months will probably draw the fewest people. Summers will be very busy, although many people may not choose to wait for the late sunset.

Nearby locations: The entire Oregon Coast is beautiful, but highlights include Cape Kiwanda State Park, with its huge waves in winter, and Bandon Beach State Park with its numerous sea stacks.

Mt. Assiniboine – British Columbia, Canada

Considered by some the most beautiful peak in North America, Mt. Assiniboine is located deep in the wilds of the Canadian Rockies. Getting there can mean a rigorous hike or an easy helicopter ride and a stay at a backcountry lodge. Whichever you choose, book early – literally years in advance for campsites or rooms at the lodge, which include meals. Backpackers should be forewarned that the hike in is long and has a moderate amount of elevation gain. The hike has special meaning for me because it proved that I could no longer do lengthy backpack trips with a 4x5 camera.

Although Mt. Assiniboine would be beautiful in winter, sadly, it faces north at its normal viewing area. Summer brings great light on the peak at both sunrise and sunset, but like most of the world's great peaks, don't expect to get a shot in one or two days there. The peak was obscured for

Mt. Assinibone at sunset

much of my visit in July and especially at sunrise and sunset. It may take several days to capture a good image, so expect to spend some time. There are many worse places to wait for good light.

One consideration at this location is the snow pack. If it's been heavy, it may be mid-July or later before it's sufficiently gone. In early July with a normal snow year, the snow was melting enough to not be a navigation problem for me, but fortunately, it was producing numerous tarns to reflect the peak all around the lodge area. The large lake there was always too rippled by wind to provide good reflections.

Though I have personally had no problem in Canada with professional-looking equipment, I've spoken with photographers who have. One was shooting with a 6x7 camera and told by a ranger to put it away or it would be confiscated.

Left: Mt. Assiniboine reflection

Maligne Lake at sunset

The Canadian Rockies – Alberta, Canada

Most of the classic photography in Banff and Jasper National Parks revolves around their stunning glacial lakes: Moraine, Peyto, Lake Louise, and Lake Maligne. You've likely seen many images of these classic subjects yourself. However, if you pay attention to the time of day and time of year, it's possible to get photos that transcend the average Lake Louise image. Most people don't realize the huge difference the angle of the sun makes in a landscape image. This is a function of the time of year.

At Moraine Lake, the classic composition is looking across the lake to the epic peaks that loom up in the distance. To have the best snow on the peaks, it would be opportune to photograph the lake as soon as the roads become navigable in late May or early June. As June progresses, the shot becomes very backlit and a late morning shot during the summer showing the blue glacial waters might be your best choice. As a general rule, the best light for the mountains is at sunrise and in the morning. As fall approaches, the mountains become side-lit at dawn. My dream shot for this location is a fall sunrise just after the first snow, when the road is still open and the lake is frozen.

Cobalt blue waters of Moraine Lake

Peyto Lake, which is viewed from high above on the Icefields Parkway, is extremely dramatic and has great light in the morning from the viewpoint during summer. Arriving in early summer when the surrounding peaks have snow, offers a great enhancement.

The lake itself turns a surreal turquoise color in late morning when the sun is high in the sky.

Lake Louise is a more difficult subject than Peyto and Moraine with their more natural settings. Early summer is once again great for the huge glaciated peak at the far end of the lake, and morning in summer is best for a classic scene as you look southwest to the peaks from the Lodge area. The wonderful lake color is the draw here, as glacial silt tints the lake a magical blue. In Jasper National Park, the Icefields Parkway traverses great scenery, especially near the Columbia Icefields. The park is also home to Maligne Lake which is exceptionally scenic at sunset and works well as a panoramic shot.

Peyto Lake

Queen Charlotte Islands – British Columbia, Canada

Rated by Lonely Planet as one of the five best places to visit in Canada, these islands offer forest wilderness and great archaeological significance. In the southernmost part of the islands, the Gwaii Haanas National Park Reserve and Haida Heritage Site are the only places in the world where visitors can see and photograph historic totem poles, over one hundred years old and in their original location. Because of the temperate rain forest conditions, totem poles created earlier have long since deteriorated.

Ancient Haida Totems, Gwaii Haanas Nat'l Park Reserve

Though totem poles are not uncommon sights in the Pacific Northwest, Alaska and British Columbia, those at Ninstints are special. Photographing them in their various stages of decay is somewhat akin to visiting Easter Island, and constitutes a genuine privilege. Getting to Ninstints is not easy, but there are guided tours and a nearby bed and breakfast in Rose Harbor, BC. When I went, the trip required flying by a commercial jet, then a smaller commuter plane, next a Cessna, and finally a motorboat. Also at Rose Harbor, a partially carved canoe of ancient vintage can be seen and photographed in the forest. The islands are known as the Galapagos of Canada for their unique flora and fauna, and the forests and mountains there offer rich potential for landscape photography.

The Alaskan Glaciers

World-renowned Alaskan Glaciers are some of the most beautiful and accessible in the world. In Southeast Alaska, Mendenhall Glacier is in close proximity to Juneau. Here you may book helicopter flights and glacial walks to ice caves, or simply drive out to the glacier yourself.

A visit to Glacier Bay National Park and Preserve requires a lot of preparation if you're going to visit by sea kayak. I have personally run treacherous rivers, visited unstable countries, and hung off more than my share of cliffs. I have even

Right: Blue glacial pool, Wrangell-St. Elias Nat'l Park

Peaks of the Wrangell Mountains

ridden with Italian taxi drivers, but sea-kayaking scares the hell out of me. I think the best way to see and photograph the Glacier Bay Glaciers—Alaska's number one most visited scenic area—is on a cruise. Princess Cruises has more sailings in Glacier Bay than anyone, and has special all-glacier cruises, which include Hubbard Glacier, College Fjord, and Prince William Sound. Trying to get around to all of these world-class sites on your own would cost a small fortune, but not on a cruise ship. Yes, you may not be there when the light is great (Alaska being notorious for overcast summers) but you will be up close and personal with many glaciers.

Another possibility is to visit McCarthy in the heart of America's biggest national park, the Wrangell-St. Elias Park and Preserve. Here some of America's highest mountains rise dramatically out of the ocean. At McCarthy, I've stayed at a great bed and breakfast close to the park entrance. From here, it's a short walk to the foot of the Root Glacier. Guided tours on Root Glacier can take you to ice caves and cobalt-blue glacial pools. If weather is good, the nearby airport has scenic flights over perhaps the best mountain scenery in North America.

A guide is recommended for glacier hikes.

The Tatshenshini River – Yukon & Alaska

The Tatshenshini River, famous for its outstanding scenery, is the premier river trip in Alaska. This wild river flows through two countries and the world's largest nature preserve. The latter is composed of two national parks plus two state and province preserves. The Tatshenshini also flows through the dramatic St. Elias Range, which has the largest elevation change from ocean to peak in the world.

All of the river trips are done in the summer when lush greenery combines with snowy peaks to make outstanding imagery. A trip on the Tatshenshini normally lasts ten days and is no different from any other river trip: camp time is free time and comes at the best time of day. One of the highlights of the trip is Glacier Bay National Park. There it's possible to spend all day hiking on Walker Glacier, filled with blue glacial pools, and deep crevasses. Near the end of the trip, you will enter Alsek Lake. Taking the trip in July will allow you to photograph Alaska's largest wildflower extravaganza there. The islands of Alsek Lake are usually covered in blooms of all kinds, with the peaks of Glacier Bay just beyond, rising two miles into the sky. Pray for good weather at this spot, and make sure your guides have left enough time for you to explore these majestic blooming islands. Also while at Alsek, have your camera ready as the rafts thread their way through icebergs calved from the many glaciers feeding the lagoon. Though your raft company will recommend what kind of clothing to bring, remember this is a river trip in sub-arctic conditions. Further, you will be entering some of the wildest country in the world. Grizzly bears are common and extremely dangerous. Do not wander far from camp alone. Mosquitoes may be a problem at times, but do not carry disease.

Access to the river is by plane and tour bus. Guides are necessary but no permit is required if you are on a guided trip. You should inform your raft company that you are bringing camera gear that needs to be kept dry.

Wildflower fields at Alsek Lake, Glacier Bay Nat'l Park

Denali (Mt. McKinley) above clouds

Denali National Park – Alaska

The focus of landscape photographers in Denali National Park is the amazing hulk of Mt. McKinley (a.k.a. Denali) itself, rising from the surrounding plains higher than almost any mountain in the world. Reflecting a theme recurring throughout this book, the problem here is that most visitors to Denali are not able to see the mountain, let alone take its picture. In the two weeks I spent there, the mountain was free of clouds for about six hours during one day. In the short summer season, when visiting Denali is feasible, there is no way to know if you will return home with an image.

Don't waste your time staying at the Princess Lodge or near the park entrance, as the mountain is not visible from either location. The best idea is to stay just outside the park or at one of the lodges or campgrounds at the end of the park road. Since private cars aren't allowed on the ninety-plus mile long dirt road to this area, you'll probably have to arrive by van. There is an airstrip nearby, however, that may make a fly-in possible. Depending on where you stay, you'll be some distance from spectacular Wonder Lake, which reflects the peak when visible. Some of the lodges, however, provide transportation to this and other great spots like the Ansel Adams Overlook. Make sure when you book your lodging that the staff are photographer-friendly, and offer someone for hire to take you to the nearby overlooks. Denali is a big chunk of real estate and can be seen, when visible, from great distances. Some of the best views outside the park are along the road leading to Denali State Park from the National Park entrance.

Aerial photography is also a great option. I consider the flight I took over Denali to be one of the most inspiring things I've ever done. I've found that shooting with a polarizer through a closed airplane window works surprisingly well, so flying with a group might be more feasible than the thousands per hour you would pay for a private charter. Naturally, being in the plane near sunset or sunrise would be the preferred option. A low level cloud deck is often the culprit in obscuring Denali, so even if you can't see the peak from the ground, you may be able to see it from above. The Denali Road and the lodging mentioned above are all primarily north of the park, offering a good sun angle during the short summer season.

Bearberry & Denali

Kilauea Volcano – Hawaii

The ever-changing and dangerous lava flows from the world's most active volcano have mesmerized and frustrated photographers from around the world for decades. Currently, the prime location for shooting the volcano is actually outside the park on a viewing platform managed by local authorities. At the time of this writing, the lava was flowing underground to the ocean and not producing any kind of a visible spectacle. This, of course, can change at any time.

Perhaps the safest and easiest way to shoot the flow into the ocean is by the lava boats departing from Hilo. Check with the companies that run these trips about recent activity. Be aware that shooting the flow during the day is not going to yield impressive images. The best times for photography are actually pre-dawn and post-sunset. At night, the lava shows up well, but there are only three colors: red, orange and black. With a little light still in the sky, the steam clouds and the ocean take on pastel colors that are much more appealing. You don't want, and likely will not receive, direct sunlight as you are in one of the wettest areas in the world. Hilo has only a few clear days a year.

I suggest visiting the area where lava is flowing into the ocean (if this is happening) at sunrise and sunset with the boats for at least a week. Each time will be different, and you will have more of a chance to capture the lava-shooter's holy grail: a lava explosion. Totally unpredictable, these firework-like displays occur with just the right mixture of rock, lava and water.

Hawaiian Waterfalls – Hawaii

With the two wettest places in the world, and the world's highest sea cliffs, the Hawaiian Islands prove the maxim that when water meets igneous rock, great cascades are born. Kauai, Molokai, Maui, and The Big Island probably have hundreds of waterfalls combined, if you include the interior cirques of Mt. Waialeale on Kauai and the West Maui Mountains. Four of the world's highest waterfalls cascade down the world's highest sea cliffs on Molokai, while the wet cliffs of the Big Island are home to a few dozen amazing falls.

There is only one way to really see and photograph all these waterfalls, and that is by helicopter. Fortunately, there are numerous opportunities to hire helicopters on the islands mentioned. When the choppers enter the interior sections of these lush green sanctums you will feel you have entered a magical kingdom.

Papalaua Falls, Molokai

Left: Lava entering Pacific Ocean

Falls tumbling into ocean, Big Island

All around you, waterfalls seem to gush from the mist. You will be so amazed that at first you may forget to photograph. I used to be very concerned about having to shoot through a closed window, but since I've used a polarizer successfully behind the helicopter glass, you should have good results, too. It is also helpful that there is rarely any direct sunlight in these locations that could create glare and reflections. At least one company uses a doorless Hughes 500 with only three passengers. It makes shooting much easier, although cameras need to be strapped. Sticking your camera outside a helicopter in the pouring rain is risky, and a filter blown-off into a rotor could be disastrous.

Remember to use a high ISO and a shutter speed of about 1/2000th. These places can be very dark, so focusing will be difficult. Your autofocus may not help much, but it's worth a try. The waterfalls on Molokai and Hawaii can be captured from a fixed-wing aircraft since they fall along a straight cliff line that does not demand much maneuvering.

The Na Pali Coast – Hawaii

The scalloped ridges of the Na Pali Coast are unique in the world. I have seen hints of this beautiful landscape structure in the Marquesas and on Cape Verde, but there is no match for the wrinkled red volcanic rock of Kauai carpeted in neon greens. At the base of the ridges are white sand beaches and beautiful blue-green ocean. To see and photograph these wonders, you can choose the easy way or the not-so-easy way, or since this is one of the world's great landscape locations, both.

The easy way simply involves driving the route past Waimea Canyon (more on this later), visiting Kokee State Park and shooting from Kalalau Valley Overlook. Summer, with the sun in the north, is best here, and the cool air at 4,000 feet is refreshing. Sunset is also great, especially if there are clouds near the ridge tops. Optionally, you can drive to the other end of Na Pali Coast and see the cliffs from Kee Beach Park. Sunset in winter is great here as the backlit cliffs are highlighted by the setting sun. Side-lighting in summer works at this locale, also. Walking up higher on the beginning of the Kalalau Trail provides a different angle for the Na Pali palisades.

Right: Na Pali Cliffs, Kauai

Double rainbow on Kalalau Beach

To reach the ultimate Na Pali photo spot, Kalalau Beach in Na Pali State Park, start with a permit which must be procured far in advance. Then, spend time at the gym on the stair climber. I believe I am one of the rare individuals to have done this extreme 22-mile round-trip hike with a 4x5 camera. When I got to Kalalau Beach surrounded on all sides with steep cliffs, a waterfall coming right into camp and the most magnificent beach in Hawaii, I knew it was worth it. I also realized that I had never seen a shot from this amazing spot by any of my colleagues. Later in the day, I was treated to the daily double rainbow show. This wonderful event happens there because the wet and dry sides of the island meet at Kalalau. The sun sets on the dry side while shining on the rainy cliffs to the east. Trying to photograph a double rainbow with a 4x5 in rain and blowing sand, with the waves moving my tripod was very difficult. It was all worth it, however, because I achieved one of the best shots of my career. I later found a couple of naked sun-bathers hiding in the 4x5 shot, par for the course at Kalalau Beach.

It is possible to get to this beach with a boat, but since a boat can't land in high surf, I was afraid I would have to swim with my 4x5 to the beach and return the same way when or if, the boat came back. People who choose this with 35mm gear might have better luck with swimming, but those who arrive by boat are told they may have to hike out anyway. My dream is to be dropped off for the day at the magnificent sea arch just down from Kalalau. I have not yet determined whether that is allowed.

Permits are required here for both hiking and camping.

Nearby locations: Waimea Canyon, on the way to Kalalau Lookout, is a beautiful eroded area of colorful volcanic soils and rocks. My best shot here, after many visits, is a panoramic from one of the first viewpoints.

❖ ❖ ❖

Agua Azul Cascades, Chiapas rainforest, Mexico

CENTRAL AMERICA
& THE CARIBBEAN

Copper Canyon at dawn

Copper Canyon – Mexico

The Copper Canyon area, once peaceful and idyllic, has unfortunately become unsafe at times due to the ongoing Mexican drug war. I include it here in hopes that things will change. Copper Canyon is an example of how an area can be safe then dangerous, then safe again, sometimes in a short period of time. Chances are you will have no problems visiting this area, but please be cautious.

Most people will only want to visit the rim of Copper Canyon, as a trip to its depths is arduous. Though not as colorful as the Grand Canyon, Copper Canyon and the surrounding area is a place of big vistas that bring to mind its northern counterpart minus the hordes of people and traffic. The area is accessible by both vehicle and train but because of the potential danger, perhaps the train is a more logical choice. The train stops at the several hotels overlooking the Canyon, which make a good base camp for further exploration. Simply walking along the rim from any of the hotels can lead you to great photo points with twisted trees as foregrounds, and huge walls dropping hundreds of feet. Like the Grand Canyon, Copper Canyon's main viewpoints are on the south rim, making it good for photography all year. Also, like its northern neighbor, the high elevation means snow in the winter and cool wet weather in the summer.

Waterfalls are common in the area and Cusarare Falls is near the town of Creel, the closest municipality to the canyon. A short walk takes you to the 100-foot falls. On a totally different scale of grandeur is Basaseachic Falls with an 800-foot drop into a Yosemite Valley-like canyon of pink granite. The falls, a national park in its own right, is most vigorous in the winter and following the huge summer monsoon rains that frequent the region. Photographing the falls from a distance and from the brink of the huge cascade are both outstanding opportunities. Morning is best from most of the primary viewpoints, which are east of Basaseachic and its canyon. Also close to Creel is the Valley of the Monks, Valley of the Frogs, and Valley of the Mushrooms, all great geologic parks with an amazing variety of subjects. With so many photographic wonders in this area, it's well worth a visit—but please remain alert for your personal safety.

Temple of the Sun, Teotihuacán

Teotihuacán – Mexico

You will read several references in this book speaking to the difficulty of photographing archaeological sites in Mexico. This is apart from the security questions that inevitably surround travel to Mexico these days. Although there are no guarantees, this is one Mexico trip that is very easy. My advice if you only wish to photograph Teotihuacán is to fly to Mexico City, stay at an airport hotel, and take a taxi to and from the pyramids. If you visit in January, which is a good time, the closing time of the ruins is fairly close to sunset. The site opens too late for sunrise, unfortunately. No tripods are allowed, so plan to use a high ISO and image stabilized lenses. Clouds are very helpful to this subject, so if you desire the best possible image, allow several days here to increase your chances of an enhanced composition. The huge Temple of the Sun is an excellent subject, with grasses, cacti, and other exotic plants to use as foreground material. A good overall view of the complex in morning light can be achieved from the top of the Temple of the Moon, shooting southwest. In the afternoon, the temple is also a great place to photograph the big pyramid, with the mountains beyond. Use your long lens for this image.

Nearby location: The ancient Toltec city of Tula in Hidalgo state is also an easy drive from an airport hotel. The attraction here is a grouping of four huge statues, quite a bit older than the pyramids. Called the Atlantean Warriors, these imposing figures are about 20 feet in height. The site was open until sunset when I visited in January. Tripods are not allowed here either.

Agua Azul Cascades

Agua Azul – Mexico

Blue-green cascades are seen in limestone-rich areas throughout the world. Agua Azul, located in Chiapas, southern Mexico, features waterfalls, blue-green cascades, and travertine sculpture. The blue-green color is best photographed on bright sunny days, and fades considerably under cloudy conditions. Use of a polarizing filter will enhance color saturation here. Unlike Mexico's archaeological parks, there was no restriction expressed by the park staff regarding my use of a tripod and professional camera.

Nearby locations: The Mayan ruins of Palenque, also in Chiapas, are among Mexico's finest. However, you will need to leave your tripod behind, push up your ISO, and use a VR (Nikon) or IS (Canon) lens. Additionally, you will not have access to the site at sunrise. In January, the closing time is approximately sunset, so it may be possible to get some good light before closing during the winter months. Temple of the Inscriptions is a wonderful small pyramid, facing straight north. Side-lighting in winter is not bad here, but summertime, early or late in the day, would be preferable.

Another blue-water wonder much further north is Havasu Canyon in the Grand Canyon. The Canyon is home to a number of turquoise waterfalls including Mooney (300 feet) and Havasu Falls, and is not part of Grand Canyon National Park.

The Mayan Ruins – Mexico

The Mayan Ruins of Mexico are another great archaeological treasure where, unfortunately, photographers with tripods are not welcome. Tripod permits are available, I understand, in Mexico City, if you wait a week and pay a large fee. To get around these seemingly impossible rules—I don't suggest you try—I did

Moonrise at Temple of the Cormorant, Dzibanche

Temple Four at Becan

things like sneaking in to Tulum along the ocean, and paying "extra" for after-hours access. Today, with new technology, tripods are not always needed, and using a higher ISO setting with image stabilization or vibration reduction can allow you to take excellent hand-held photos. Camera technology advances will not, of course, impact limited hours of operation at the major ruins.

Tulum, along the Caribbean coast, is a favorite site of mine due to its location: a great beach front on a typically tropical blue

Bougainvillea at Temple of the Sun, Konichna

The Great Pyramid at Calakmul

stretch of ocean. To get this shot, walk all the way to the southern perimeter of the ruins and shoot to the north. Midday is fine, but I would love to be at Tulum at sunrise with some great tropical clouds. Unfortunately, it will never happen.

The finest Mayan pyramid in Mexico is at Palenque, a huge complex in Chiapas State. The pyramid faces north, so being there on a summer morning would be best.

Chichén Itzá has a very impressive ball court, the largest of all the Mayan sites. It also has a great pyramid, El Castillo, but ongoing excavations and crowds make it almost impossible to photograph without major Photoshop post-processing. It is the most visited archaeological site in Mexico; the redeeming factor being that some hotels are located next to the site, with a private entrance. I also like Uxmal's stepless Pyramid of the Magician, with its unusual rounded corners.

Some lesser-known ruins of the Yucatan Peninsula are almost as mind-blowing as the well known and crowd-filled sites, and have fewer guards. I was able to take my tripod and 4x5 to the top of the Calakmul Pyramid in Campeche for sunset and no one seemed to care. This view of the jungle in the Calakmul Biosphere Preserve from the largest single Pre-Columbian structure is beyond description. Other Mayan ruins where guards might allow you to visit outside normal hours and even use tripods, include Dzibanche, Konichna (no guards at all when I visited), and Becan (especially Temple Four).

Permits are required and tripods are only rarely allowed at the Mayan sites.

The Blue Hole – Belize

The jewel of the Mesoamerican Reef, a huge coral reef system second only in size to the Great Barrier Reef, is the perfectly round Blue Hole. This unique location was brought to the world's attention by the Cousteau expeditions. An example of a landscape subject that can only be adequately photographed from above, it's necessary to hire a light plane or helicopter in Belize City and fly out to the Hole, located about fifty miles from the mainland. A polarizing filter is helpful here.

I was fortunate enough to arrive at the Hole when no dive boats were there, although they can add the element of scale. Full mid-day sunlight is by far the best for this shot. There were quite a few clouds in the area, but none casting a shadow on the Hole when I visited. I believe clouds build up frequently in this tropical area, and become more numerous in the afternoon. Considering that, a late morning visit would increase your chances here.

Besides the Blue Hole, there is a great shipwreck on the reef just to the north which is another great aerial photographic opportunity.. There are also many great reef patterns in the north part of nearby Lighthouse Reef.

Aerial view of the Blue Hole

Tikal, Temples I, II, & III seen from Temple IV

Tikal – Guatemala

Being a huge movie fan myself, many of the places I visit are inspired by a location I've seen on screen. I'm still trying to find the location of the amazing Chinese hills in Hero, one of the best landscape movies ever made. My first glimpse of Tikal was in the original Star Wars movie. I beat Steven Spielberg to Petra, but George Lucas beat me to Guatemala.

My trip to Tikal came very early in my travels, and my flight was late arriving there. Instead of staying at the hotel on the grounds of Tikal as planned, I had to commute 50 or so miles each way to the site. This meant no foggy sunrises like I had seen in the shots of others. Fog happens a lot at Tikal, especially in the winter, so arrive at the park early for this effect. I did enjoy beautiful clouds there, which were great for the Jaguar Temple, and some of the other sites. My favorite composition is Temples I, II, and III protruding above the endless jungle as photographed at sunset from the top of Temple IV. Unlike the Mayan ruins in Mexico, the guards at Tikal placed no restrictions on photography when I visited. I hope that hasn't changed.

Nearby location: The great portrait stelae (carved tablets) of Copán, Honduras, are the best in the Mayan world.

Temple I (Jaguar Temple)

Arenal Volcano eruption

Arenal Volcano – Costa Rica

Arenal Volcano puts on quite a show, and it's probably the easiest-to-photograph active volcano in the world. Like most volcano photography, night is the preferred time. For a viewpoint, nothing beats the Arenal Observatory Lodge, where you can shoot the volcano from the deck of your room (specify a room facing the volcano).

Focus critically on your composition before dark, and remember dark comes quickly in the tropics. Set your camera for high ISO and if your camera has a noise-reduction feature, you may wish to use that also. Remember that on many cameras the in-camera noise reduction only works on jpegs. Arenal's eruptions consist not of lava, but of hot red boulders that roll down the slopes. Like most volcanoes, Arenal is unpredictable, but does tend to follow a pattern, at times. Using a cable release, I opened the shutter when the eruption became visible at the top of the volcano. I left the shutter open as long as I could, usually around 90 seconds at f/4, with an ISO of 1250 (depending on noise generated by your sensor, this may vary). Having shot Arenal in both the winter and summer, I much prefer the summer with its foggy mists surrounding the eruptive peak.

This adds another element of other-worldly mystique. My images with fog made me think of Venus.

As of this writing, Arenal has gone into a quiet period. As I mentioned, however, volcanoes are unpredictable and this one could roar back to life at any time.

The Costa Rica Rainforest

Rainforests pose some problems for landscape photographers, but since they are such an important part of the world's natural systems, it's always fun to try to capture rainforest images that impart some of the beauty of these lush, green spaces. One of the best places to photograph rainforests is Costa Rica, a place with many national parks and private jungles that are easy to visit and photograph.

Roads from San Jose lead to Braulio Carillo National Park. Here you will find great vistas of forest-covered montane and trails that penetrate the rainforest. Monteverde Cloudforest Preserve features streams and waterfalls that help break up the sometimes oppressive green. La Selva Biological Station trails lead to "natural arch" fig trails that form doorways through the trees and overgrown wooden bridges nature has reclaimed. My favorite location in Costa Rica is El Toro Waterfall in Castro National Park. From this falls, full of water in summer, you can see the low-hanging clouds over the distant Central Volcanic Range and its wild canyons of virgin rainforest.

Toro Waterfall, Juan Castro Nat'l Park

Many people think Costa Rica is best in winter. I prefer summer though, when the forests are a dozen shades of green and the waterfalls are strong. If you proceed higher in altitude, the daily rains offer cool temperatures even in June and July. Some photographers have difficulty keeping their equipment dry and have issues with condensation, so take measures to shield your gear and avoid rapid changes from air conditioned buildings to the warm, humid outdoors. During the summer, clouds and overcast weather will be predominant. These are perfect conditions for rainforest photography.

Nearby locations: Manuel Antonio National Park and Corcovado National Park, both on the Pacific Coast, offer spectacular tropical forest scenery and fauna.

The Baths, Virgin Gorda – British Virgin Islands

Beaches surrounded by majestic boulders have always appealed to travelers and photographers. The Seychelles are great, but just as appealing and easier to get to, the Baths of Virgin Gorda combine golden sand beaches, sculpted granite boulders and blue Caribbean waters. A polarizing filter is conducive here, and midday is best for sand and water color. The Baths is not a large area, and it's easy to find some great locations among the boulders. Also, getting to the beach in late morning before the cruise ship shuttles arrive is a good idea. The beaches become very crowded in the afternoon, all year.

Access is by boat or car. Remember, use sun block.

Small beach between boulders, The Baths

Nearby location: A majestic viewpoint and photo location gives a celebrated view of Trunk Bay with its beach and lagoon, and is located just off the road. The site, in the U.S. Virgin Islands National Park on St. John, is usually loaded with visitors in early afternoon when the light is best. They can be easily removed in Photoshop, however, if desired. The location is truly a classic view on the North Shore Road.

The Pitons, St. Lucia Island

The Pitons – Saint Lucia

The two Piton peaks rising out of the blue Caribbean dominate the island of St. Lucia and can be easily photographed by visiting this beautiful paradise. From Castries, the road climbs up the mountains and heads south. After an hour's drive, you will reach great viewing areas of the Pitons, right along the highway. A summer sunrise or sunset would create the best lighting here, but with nice tropical clouds and the beautiful green forests, midday shots at any time of year could hold appeal. Boat tours also approach the Pitons from the ocean. This would be preferable in the afternoon or at sunset. There are some beaches below the peaks that make great foregrounds.

Bottom Beach – Barbados

Picking the most photogenic beaches in the Caribbean is tough, but Bottom Beach in Barbados definitely stands out. Sports Illustrated thinks so too, conducting a lot of swimsuit photography there over the years. Here, you won't be bothered by the crowds normally associated with beautiful beaches. My taxi driver told me he hadn't taken anyone there for years.

Bottom Beach

Morning is a great time, as puffy clouds begin to form over the turquoise water. I consider tropical water to be like shooting in slot canyons back home. Midday definitely beats the standard magic hour paradigm in this case. Sunrise and sunset give the water a rather muddy color, while shooting when the sun is high allows the light to bounce off the white coral bottom and create the great blue that David Gilmour and Enya sing about. Polarizers are also effective in taking away the water's sheen and delivering pure color. One of the key components of a great beach scene to me, is the presence of palm trees. You'd be surprised how many great beaches just don't work because the palm trees can't be integrated into the shot. At Bottom Beach, a high ridge on the level of the parking lot puts you right in the middle of the palms, with the beach and ocean beyond. Working along the ridge gives you a number of great possibilities and blocks the people in the alcove below with their kiosks and loungers.

Nearby location: A few miles away from Bottom Beach is Crane Beach and although it's developed, it's quite beautiful. A little bit farther along, South Point Lighthouse is a bright orange-striped beauty, although it's a little rusty and has seen better days. It can be photographed from underneath, or you may drive down below the lighthouse to a beautiful hillside garden that provides great foreground.

Beech Tree at Salto Grande, Torres del Paine Nat'l Park

SOUTH AMERICA

Angel Falls

Canaima National Park – Venezuela

I was very impressed with Canaima National Park in Venezuela. Imagine Zion National Park with 2,000 foot waterfalls raining down everywhere you look. One of the highest of these is Angel Falls. The lost-world character of Canaima coupled with impenetrable jungle, rushing rivers and a lack of people is spell-binding.

The problem with photographing Angel Falls itself is timing. You will want the falls to be flowing strongly. Unfortunately, if there is too much water volume (all tours go to the falls by boat), the area becomes inaccessible. Simply put, it's a crapshoot, but one I was lucky to win the first time I visited. My trip was during the first week in September, towards the end of the wet season when water levels are dropping but rain is still recharging the falls. Trips to the falls require at least two overnight stays, so you will be camping beside the rivers with 'tepui' (giant mesas) all around. The chances for trophy images here are very good.

A good shot of Angel Falls can be made from the former campground nearby (too bad it's no longer in use). This is also the location where your boat will dock for the hike to the Falls. You will have to walk around a little bit to find the best vantage point. Don't take too much time, because your fairly long climb to the main falls viewpoint should begin soon after arrival. Going straight up from the campground, the hour long hike is strenuous and can be slippery. Exercise caution. Usually groups are given an hour or two at the main viewpoint before heading down. Be advised that arrival at the viewpoint does not guarantee a photo, as fog can come in at any time and spoil your chances.

Don't miss other falls in the region on your way back. Most trips include an aerial flight in an ancient propeller plane. If they flew over the falls, this would be great, but instead they try to get as close to the falls as possible—very scary. If your Spanish is good, you might be able to talk one of the many small aircraft pilots that land at the park entrance to take you over the falls.

Caño Cristales – Colombia

The miracle of Caño Cristales has been hidden from the world until very recently. Deep in the jungles of the Columbian Llano, the canyon and its charms were recently a main center of activity for the FARC guerilla group, known for ruthless kidnappings and narco-terrorism. In their place on my recent visit, a large contingent of Columbian soldiers protects the sudden surge of visitors to this world-class photographic phenomenon.

Several factors must come together to create the amazing colors of the stream at Caño Cristales. Most important are the crystal clear waters coming from springs fed by wet season rains. From December until July, there's nothing here to see but some great waterfalls. With the rising waters in July, the perennial underwater plants, Macarenia clavigera, start to flower with colors ranging through every shade of purple and violet to bright red. If the plants are covered with too much water early in the season, they can't be seen. If the water drops

Colors at Caño Cristales

Julia butterflies drinking from Caño Cristales

from lack of rain, they look awful. Timing is critical and the river can rise or drop substantially in a short period of time.

Besides the colors of the underwater plants, the river bed has an intense yellow mineral color, probably stained by tannic acid. This is an effect I have seen at other locations in South America. This oily looking substance also creates fantastic reflections, adding shades of blue to the mix if the sky is clear. Another color is added by the orange rocks of the streambed.

Finally, like coral reefs and slot canyons, the colors of Caño Cristales look best when the sun is high overhead and brightly penetrating the waters. Getting a sunny day during the tropical rainy season may be easier said than done. When I visited, I received just one sunny day. I actually deleted the shots I had taken on the previous cloudy day because there was no comparison in color saturation. One of the guides said the sun had not been out for weeks. The fickle nature of this locale can be observed in my own experience: day one provided clouds and good water levels, day two provided sun and good water levels, and day three had water levels too low to shoot the flowering plants. On day four when I was leaving, there was quite a lot of rain, which may have brought the levels up. This scenario took place in late August.

A guide is required for Caño Cristales.

Right: Underwater plants

San Agustín Archaeological Park – Colombia

South America is rich with photogenic archaeology. The best photos of these amazing historical places should evoke the magic and mystery of Native American culture. San Agustín is one of the lesser known sites. Although not famous, I believe San Agustín deserves inclusion here for its uniqueness, and for the welcoming attitude the government of Colombia extends toward serious photographers.

The park exists where ancient statues, no two alike, are surrounded by the looming Andes and the equatorial jungle. It's this unique setting that really speaks to some people, who return to the park again and again. There is one logistical hurdle to overcome, however. To protect the statues, they are often covered by everything from small umbrella-like structures to complete open-air roofs. With some of the carvings, this works well, providing flat lighting most of the day. More problematic is trying to use the surrounding mountains in the shot without including fencing and coverings. You will see that with a little Photoshop retouching plus HDR or a GND filter, you can overcome this hurdle.

San Agustín Park is really spread out over several locations. The main park is divided into Mesitas A, B and C, plus the Forest of the Statues trail. Mesita A offers one of the best sunset figures in the park. Though it doesn't have a name that I could find, you will see the figure on the left as you enter from the gate. It's in the perfect position for late light with the Andes beyond. Mesita B is mainly a

Ancient statue at San Agustin

morning locale, with one of my favorite statues, the Sun God (in need of dental work), facing east. Try to arrive at this location as early as possible in the morning, to shoot the somewhat creepy Midwife. The Forest Trail visits many interesting works, including the Rain God, who features a rainbow coming from his hands. This figure is considered the most artistic work in the park. The Forest Trail also provides some spotlight effects during the long tropical mid-day. An HDR approach may work here.

Some statues have interesting rainforest trees surrounding them that would look good in flat light, common here in the summer rainy season. San Agustín also includes the Mountain of the Idols Park which boasts the famous Erich Von Däniken "Headphones Man", the largest statue of all at over 30 meters in height.

Sun God statue

San Agustín opens at 9 AM and closes at dark. The rangers there allowed me in before the standard opening time, however.

Machu Picchu – Peru

The breathtaking spectacle of Machu Picchu on its island-in-the-sky perch below the Andes and above the Urubamba River is unique in the world. It is South America's most visited tourist attraction.

To shoot the classic view of the ruins from the hill above at the Funerary Rocks requires some planning and good fortune. First, try to visit Machu Picchu when the sun is in the south, or during the austral summer. You will be looking straight north and the scene is otherwise backlit during the Northern Hemisphere's summer. Second, it's important to be in place at about 5:00 am. To do this will probably require camping above the ruins on the Inca Trail, or staying at the expensive hotel adjacent to the site and persuading the guards to allow you entry. I did the latter, but was lodged at the former hotel, which was more rustic and less expensive. Many people from the hotel were let into the grounds after I came in, and I believe the guests still enjoy those privileges. To pay as much as you do for the hotel there, you ought to receive some perks. Besides catching the great morning light, which I think is preferable to the afternoon or evening illumination, you will avoid the thousands of people the buses quickly disgorge as they roll in from below.

Machu Picchu, lost city of the Incas

Something I haven't tried is walking up pre-dawn from down below. The ancient trail is steep and dangerous even during the day, and would become more so in the dark. This approach would be risky. My suggestion of visiting the site in summer puts you there during the rainy season, so I recommend visiting for a period of several days to wait for good light. You may also get fog around the ruins or the nearby peaks. This effect creates a great mood for an ancient ruin.

Once you've tired of shooting the big scenic—if that's possible—there are still many detail shots and other photo possibilities to explore: windows framing the ruin or the mountains, amazing multi-ton stone blocks carved and fitted with precision, and interesting roofless interiors receiving full natural light.

Llama at Machu Picchu

Also, llamas can sometimes be found foraging at the upper part of the site, and seem to be quite accustomed to photographers. These are always interesting subjects and look even better with Inca ruins as background.

Although guards didn't stop me from shooting with a tripod, there has been a change in policy in recent years. Apparently, large equipment such as full-frame DSLRs, long zooms, and tripods are now subject to a permit—as well as a very high fee. An acquaintance reported being stopped by a ranger wanting to know if he sold his work, and demanding that he ceased photographing unless he returned with a permit. Many people have reported similar incidents on travel and photography forums; some describe smuggling camera and tripod in inconspicuous backpacks and keeping an eye out for guards. You're on your own.

The Nazca Lines – Peru

I'm always amazed when someone tells me they've never heard of the Nazca Lines. After all, they are the world's largest and most extensive geoglyphs. I personally find them to be on the scale of the world's greatest archeological wonders. Recent discoveries about the Nazca culture have found it to be one of the oldest in the New World.

The term "lines" is a bit of a misnomer. There are long lines involved, but the most amazing geoglyphs are huge figures of hummingbirds, spiders, monkeys, cranes, and other animals and patterns. They were created by removing the top layer of dark soil to reveal the lighter layer underneath. The fact that the lines can be most easily seen from the air led to many silly theories that they were extra-terrestrial in origin. I enjoy pondering aliens as much as the next guy, but scientists have found that almost all the figures can be easily seen from the surrounding plateaus and mountains.

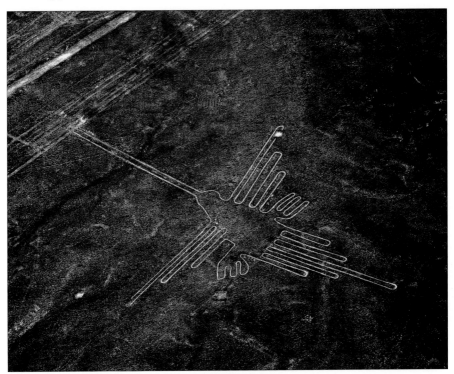

The Hummingbird

For photographs, however, airplanes are the way to go, and the airport at Nazca is fully equipped to take you up for a great view. On my two visits to Nazca, I have chartered a plane for myself, so I can get the exact angle I want. Please refer to the section on aerial photography in the introduction for some tips and guidelines on this unique type of photography. The sun is always shining in Nazca, so you will have sunny weather and fortunately, this is one site that works well in bright sun. The heavy shadows of early or late light would only detract from the subject. Most flights go in the late morning before the desert sun brings thermals, which create turbulence. This makes it difficult for the photographer to maintain steadiness and the contents of their stomach.

Nazca is a little challenging to get to. It is possible to catch a charter flight from Lima, but I have used the comfortable bus service available as there are no regularly scheduled flights.

Other geoglyphs of photographic interest include the Giant of the Atacama, the world's largest prehistoric art figure, 800 miles south of Nazca. Though a shot from an airplane would make the best image, it is possible to shoot the giant from the ground. Like many geoglyphs in the Atacama, it is not on flat ground but cut into a hillside. The Giant somewhat resembles crop-circle art, and is truly amazing.

The Atacama Desert & the Altiplano – Chile & Bolivia

Except for a few trickles that flow through from the Andes Mountains, the Atacama Desert is the driest on Earth. How dry is it? There are no insects, no lichens and no native plants or animals of any kind except a few birds that might find themselves flying over. Antarctica is teeming with life compared to the Atacama.

The starkness of the desert alone is a great subject, but most photographers will be drawn to the Valley of the Moon, an area of erosion-gone-crazy near San

Pedro de Atacama. Like most desert landscapes, sunrise and sunset are best here, and the sun is always visible at those times. With scenery somewhat reminiscent of the American Southwest, this desert land-scape has dazzling red cliffs, rock pinnacles, balanced rocks and snow-covered peaks in the distance. The big difference is the lack of trees, which is great in some ways because nothing blocks your ability to see at the many viewpoints. If you can

Valley of the Moon at dawn

Laguna Verde & Licancabur Volcano

get the moon in your shot, (usually best one day before the full moon) it adds a prosaic touch.

From your base in San Pedro de Atacama, an early morning tour of the El Tatio geyser field offers interesting sunrise shots.

With a full day, it's easy to cross into Bolivia to photograph the turquoise waters of Laguna Verde with the conical shape of Volcán Licancabur in the background. With two days, you can push to the red salt flats of Laguna Colorada and its myriads of Pink Flamingos, wander around the Sol de Mañana geothermal area, and photograph the impossibly balanced Árbol de Piedra.

Take three days and see all of the above on your way to the fantastic Salar de Uyuni—the world's largest salt flat. The immense Salar has spectacular "islands": rocky outcrops covered with native cacti; the best are Isla de Pescados and Isla Incahuasi.

A guide/driver and a 4WD vehicle is a necessity in Bolivia. Lodging along the way ranges from simple 'refugio' to relatively comfortable hotels. Be sure you've taken a few days to acclimatize before venturing on the Altiplano, or you'll be hit with a massive case of 'soroche' (altitude sickness).

Nearby locations: If time is limited or you'd rather not cross into Bolivia, you can get a taste of the Altipano at Laguna Miscanti, with Volcan Miscanti in the background and great herds of vicuñas. This trip can be done easily in an afternoon from San Pedro with a 4WD rental, or with a guide/driver.

Árbol de Piedra

Isla Incahuasi

Further north, at the Chilean/Peruvian/Bolivian border lies another highly photogenic gem of the Altiplano: Lauca National Park. There is a lot to shoot in this World Biosphere Reserve: the photogenic Andean village of Parinacota, herds of vicuñas and llamas on the shores of Laguna Chungara (the highest large lake in the world at 15,000+ feet) and the spectacular shape of Volcan Parinacota. Lauca can be visited easily in one full day with a guide/driver or rental car from Arica; you'll be going from sea level to 15,000 feet in less than 3 hours—a trip so fast that most day-visitors don't even have time to get sick.

Vicuñas & Volcán Parinacota

Ischigualasto Provincial Park – Argentina

The great desert areas of South America are often overlooked for a simple reason: the Andes and the Amazon Basin receive all the attention. Deserts occur in many South American countries, and Argentina has one of the most scenic and photogenic examples. Besides great rock formations and outstanding desert scenery, the Andes are always looming to the west, and can sometimes be

Round concretions at Cancho de Bochas

incorporated into your composition. My personal favorite is actually a World Heritage Site, Ischigualasto Provincial Park in Argentina.

For some reason, any desert land in South America is automatically tagged with the name, 'Valley of the Moon'. I think Argentina has two areas by that name, one in the north and the other in Patagonia in the far south. The park has three great areas that make wonderful sunset subjects. The first of these is 'The Submarine' and its adjacent natural arch, ideal for framing the composition there. The second sunset subject is 'The Bowling Balls', an area of amazing round concretions cast about a plain. Finally, the third is the 'El Hongo Balanced Rock', backed by a wall of sandstone that blazes as red as

El Hongo balanced rock

any similar feature on the Colorado Plateau, in the United States.

I visited Ischigualasto in the middle of summer and although it was warm, there were no bugs and no other people.

Aconcagua – Argentina

Aconcagua sunrise

The highest peak in the Western Hemisphere, Mt. Aconcagua is perhaps the easiest of the Seven Summits to see and photograph. In summer, make a pre-dawn trip to the pass between Santiago, Chile and Mendoza, Argentina. Turn off at the main park entrance which is near the top of the pass. A parking area at the end of the road in the Horcones Valley is surrounded by meadows and glacial ponds that make great reflections of the peak at sunrise. You'll see the towering mountains from here in the distance. The summit is so high it gets light very early, so be there and ready to shoot in advance of the light. Remember the light is over two miles above you, so bracketing for HDR or using a GND filter is a good strategy to consider here.

Nearby location: The very colorful travertine formations of the Puente del Inca hot springs.

Osorno Volcano & the Lake District, Chile & Argentina

Somewhat reminiscent of the Pacific Northwest in America, the Chilean/ Argentinean Lake District is home to numerous lakes, waterfalls and snow-capped volcanoes. In recent years, some of the perfectly formed volcano cones have produced some other-worldly and visually stunning eruptions. Unfortunately, you would have to be extremely lucky to catch one of these in the act.

Osorno Volcano in Pérez Rosales National Park is one of the premier places to go for landscape photography in the region. The perfect cone of the volcano can be seen from the Pétrohue Waterfalls, making a wonderful composition in the afternoon. Reflections on Llanquihue Lake are tough because the lake is so large, but I found little coves with still water in summer, to capture this shot. For interesting foreground material, consider the pampas grasses and lava flows found there.

The Lake District continues east all the way to Nahuel Huapi National Park and San Carlos de Bariloche in Argentina. The Lake District area is also well-known for its fall foliage.

Right: Pétrohue Falls & Volcán Osorno

Sunrise on the Torres del Paine

Torres del Paine National Park – Chile

I've heard Torres del Paine described as the most beautiful national park land-scape in South America. I could not argue with that premise.

Beauty aside, I have no 4x5 images of Torres because of the almost relentless summer wind there. Continual pouring rain made shooting with my Pentax 6x7 the best alternative during my visit. In the week I spent there during January, most of my time was inside a tent reading Tolstoy. To illustrate the winds power at Torres, consider the following: I was set up to photograph a field of wildflow-ers, peaks behind them, on a rare cloudless day, yet somehow rain seemed to be constantly falling from a clear blue sky. After some time, it became apparent to me that the "rain" was really water blown from the surface of a lake, several miles away. Some photographers have found that the wind problem is reduced in fall and winter, and in spite of my earlier statements, I have seen photographs of the lakes in the park with perfect reflections.

Lago Pehoe, one of the many glacial blue-green lakes is a good base of opera-tions for the park. You can camp there or stay at the comfortable Hosteria Pehoe. Pehoe affords good views of the entire range, although in winter the mountains would be backlit. One of the best viewpoints for the Cuernos is near the road leading to the ultra-expensive Explora Lodge. From there, a thin peninsula breaks Lago Pehoe, creating the appearance of two lakes for a more dynamic shot. Besides the Cuernos, or horns, that can be easily seen from all vantage points, the interior of the range has some large, even spikier peaks. I hiked up into the range from the east side one day, to shoot them from below. A similar shot can be taken on the northeast side of the range from a hike to the Mirador Las Torres. Sunrise or morning is the best time for this, so camping or staying on this side of the range works best. With a long telephoto, good shots of the spiky peaks can also be taken from the Laguna Azul area, but a four-wheel drive vehicle might be needed to reach this location. At the south end of the park road is Lago Grey,

Lago Pehoe & the Cuernos

a glacier-fed lake with milky water and some imposing bluish icebergs floating around; the best vantage point to photograph them is from the east side of the small island at the end of the beach. If you visit in summer or winter, bring all your rain gear and warm clothes. While I was there, the wind was responsible for the death of several Japanese campers who could not set up their tent in the gale. I've been to Antarctica and Torres in summer, and I think Antarctica was warmer.

Los Glaciares National Park – Argentina

A cobalt blue glacier face and my pick for one of the most beautiful mountains in the world are the two main draws in this great Patagonian park. The peak

Perito Moreno glacier

Cerro Fitzroy sunrise

is Mt. Fitzroy, standing high above the Patagonian plains. If not obscured by clouds, it is absolutely stunning at dawn.

A short steep hike is required to take you from Campamento Poincenot to the Laguna de los Tres viewpoint, with great views of the spiky mountain stronghold above the lakes. A longer hike requiring camping and using horses is possible. This will take you to higher, small lakes with great reflections. The problem at Mt. Fitzroy is the problem with many great peaks of the world that are almost constantly obscured by clouds. I hiked up to the first viewpoint every day for two weeks and never secured a sunrise shot. I did see the peaks revealed for a few minutes one morning outside the envelope of good light, but that was it. The other problem, if you're visiting in summer as I was, is the strong wind in Patagonia (called the "Broom of God" by the locals) that is related to the cloud cover. This situation is also discussed in the entry on Torres del Paine. Some have suggested visiting in the fall or winter, when the high pressure off the South American Coast breaks down a little and winds subside somewhat. Galen Rowell's famous climb and photographs of these peaks took place in winter. During winter there are other problems however: lakes are frozen, trails may be icy, and support businesses in nearby El Chaltén may be closed. Fall (April-May) might be the best time of all, with fewer people, more clear days on the mountain and most services still in place. As with lots of mountain photography, luck is a big factor.

The other great photo-op from El Chaltén is the impossibly steep mile-high spire of Cerro Torre, using the emerald green waters and floating ice of Laguna Torre to frame the shot. The hike to Mirador Laguna Torre and back is a moderate 15-miler, or you can camp below the lake at Campamento de Agostini.

Rich blue 'Penitentes' of the Perito Merono glacier

Having good light at Moreno Glacier, the other highpoint of Los Glaciares, seemed to be much easier to come by. From the standard viewpoint, summer afternoons and evenings offer good side-lighting with the face of the glacier in shade (therefore more blue) and the tortured expanse of the glacier beyond. Although the face of the glacier changes, it normally faces southeast, and will be fully lit in summer morning light. Though you will undoubtedly have some clouds, the sun should appear sufficiently to give you some excellent results. Due to the bright snow, contrast can be a problem here. This can be solved with HDR or a GND filter.

Iguazu Falls – Brazil & Argentina

One of South America's biggest tourist destinations, Iguazu Falls, is perhaps the world's greatest cascade. Though the trail on the Brazil side of the falls is only one kilometer long, I spent a week shooting there. Every day, sunrise, and sunset were different.

Sunset light on Iguazu Falls

Garganta del Diablo, from the Argentina side

Just beyond the front steps of the Hotel das Cataratas (which I recommend, by the way) there's a viewpoint of the falls that glows red at sunrise and lights up with the setting sun. Walking out on the platform above the falls reveals an amazing rainbow in the early morning, another great shot. With the water full of tannic acid, it has a slight reddish color, further enhanced by sunset light. The observation tower and platforms at the end of the trail also lead to spectacular shots, but the constant spray makes it difficult to shoot. I also did helicopter aerial shots at Iguazu, which is the only way to show the true magnitude of the falls. Visiting as I did in September (October works too) has its advantages: humidity is low, crowds are small and prices are lower. The falls is not at its peak flow at this time, but I think too much water would be less appealing, photographically.

I flew to the falls from Sao Paulo and stayed on the Brazilian side (hired cars can take you across the border to the Argentine side). During the week I spent on the Brazil side, I was never bothered by authorities while shooting with my 4x5 camera. Within minutes of striking out on the trail on the Argentine side, I was approached by a ranger asking for a permit. He said he was going to "arrest" me, but was called away on other urgent business. I'm told that photographing with less visible equipment would not draw such ire. The trail network on the Argentine side is quite extensive with a lower trail and an upper trail, a very short "ferry" crossing to an island, and a narrow-gauge train to the highlight of the Argentinean side: the Garganta del Diablo. For the Garganta, I would recommend catching the last train out to get the best light. The view is so vast, taking a number of shots for stitching might be the best option. In the evening, great flocks of noisy parrots take advantage of the massive air currents to perform aerobatics in the huge abyss. The rangers will shoo you out so there is no risk of missing the last train back. The Sheraton on the Argentine side doesn't have the old charm of the Brazilian hotel and is very pricy, but it is right at the beginning of the trail. Trails close at night and reopen early in the morning, so you'll have a good thirty minutes to yourself before the onslaught of visitors coming from outside the park.

Left: Cloud rays at Iguazu Falls, Brazil side

Rio De Janeiro – Brazil

I've been very fortunate with my photo travels across the globe. The reason I'm able to continue funding these trips myself, is that I seem to always capture enough good, commercially viable images to pay for the trips and more. This comes with both stock photo and gallery sales.

I include this entry because Rio de Janeiro is important by its own merit, but represents an example of a photo trip that has failed for me. As you attempt to photograph some of the places in this book, you may fail as well. It's a horrible feeling to travel so far, and to devote so much time and money to a job which you desperately hope to accomplish, only to come back empty-handed. It is little consolation that the fault is usually not your own. That was the case with the Rio image I had in mind.

I wasn't really trying for anything new, but I arrived to a week of rain and a famous statue, my intended subject, covered in scaffolding. The shot I wanted was of the huge statue of Christ the Redeemer with the city and ocean behind it, far below. After two days of scouting, I realized that the only way to capture my composition was from a helicopter. Ground shots were just not going to suffice in this case. Fortunately, helicopter tours of the statue are readily available there. So learning from my mistakes, should I ever return, I would do the following: 1) copy the standard shot that appears in the movie Fast Five; 2) arrive to shoot in the winter with the sun in the north and less chance of rain; 3) join a sunrise helicopter tour of the city; or 4) charter a helicopter for the short flight to the 'Redeemer' at dawn.

If this classic view of the city is not so important to you, there are many places where you can get great city shots without the Redeemer as the centerpiece. The view from the Sugarloaf, is exceptional for one, and can be an excellent twilight scene. The Sugarloaf is accessible by gondola.

Diamantina National Park – Brazil

If you've dreamed of climbing a Venezuelan Tepui and gazing down on Angel Falls, Diamantina National Park can almost replicate that experience with less trouble, danger, and expense. A land of smaller mesas in Brazil, Diamantina is also home to some of the most psychedelic colored waters on the planet. Diamantina resembles a Southwestern landscape covered by forest, but with water stained by yellow and red tannins in one place and colored turquoise by limestone in others.

Fumaca waterfall, at 1,700 feet in height, should be your first destination. Like Angel Falls, luck and timing are everything. If you visit during the wet season in the summer, the roads in the area may be impassable, though the waterfall will be flowing at its maximum. Visiting on the cusp of the season might be a better choice with good rain but no flooding. It rains a lot in Diamantina, except in the winter. Because of poor infrastructure, lack of signage and poor roads, a guide

Rainwater pools on mesa top, Diamantina Nat'l Park

is necessary for this site. With your guide, the trip to the falls is an all day hike, and can be a long, slippery, uphill trek. As your approach the edge of the mesa, the waters pool up above the falls--blood red in some places and yellow in others. You will start shooting on the right hand side of the falls. This view shows the stunning size of the drop. If the water is not prohibitively deep, you can cross and shoot on the other side, closer to the lip of the cascade. Stay behind the ropes, as stray breezes from the falling water can be very dangerous. Several Brazilians with me at this spot were sure "The gringo is going to die".

Visiting the famous blue pools at Blue Cave shows off the other side of Diamantina. This requires only a drive and a short walk. Sunlight enters the cave only between April and September from 10:30 to 12:30 in the morning. Mount Pai Ignacio is a great sunset location with views in all directions of the park, and requires only a short walk. If there has been recent rain, you may find water pockets filled with blood-red water colored by tannic acid. A guide is recommended here.

Historic center, Salvador de Bahia

Salvador Old Town, Bahia – Brazil

With multi-colored buildings, the old town of Salvador is the most beautiful historic district in South America. Spanish colonial buildings and churches are painted green, blue, yellow, red and orange—a kaleidoscope of color.

The classic shot in Salvador is of the small area of "Pelourinho", as it is referred to in Brazilian Portuguese. The best approach here is to shoot down the street from the broad open area above the colored buildings. A fair amount of sky will be included, so the presence of clouds is a big plus to the composition. HDR is also helpful to bring out detail in the shadowed buildings on the right. Around the equinoxes, sunlight illuminates the left hand buildings in the morning, which is also the best time to shoot the area without crowds. Shooting during the summer months will place the sun at your back, with the opposite occurring in the afternoon. At times during the winter months, the scene will become backlit and difficult to expose evenly. Detail shots of this World Heritage Site are also a great idea. Salvador has a bad reputation for crime. I stayed in a nice boutique hotel just a block from the best part of Old Town, and set up my tripod right next to the police station.

A guide is recommended here.

The Amazon River – Brazil

There are many ways to explore the Amazon River. Along with the Sahara Desert, it is one of the largest tracts of wilderness covered in this book. I will put forward one comfortable and safe way to visit a place that can otherwise be very dangerous, and it's a good strategy for taking photos there, as well. However you decide to visit the Amazon, it will involve a boat.

I'm going to assume that your base of operations for Amazon exploration will be the city of Manaus, Brazil. Any Amazon photo venture should start with a short trip by small boat to January Lake, an area flooded by the Amazon that is famous for giant water lilies. This is one of the main subjects I hoped to photograph there. Unfortunately, when I visited, the river had reached historic highs and ripped all the water lilies out by their roots for that season. More were growing back, and I intend to return to Manaus to photograph them. I was told they reach their peak around mid-summer.

Sunset on the Amazon, near Rio Negro

Huge kapok tree

My second recommendation is a cruise with a reputable company up the Rio Negro, a tributary of the Amazon. The water in the Rio Negro is black from tannic acid, and makes a great reflective surface for photography. The natural chemical also keeps mosquitoes and other insects at bay—diminishing risks of malaria and dengue fever. If you pick one of the good tour companies, you travel in a small group, remain safe at night from animals and insects, and enjoy good safe meals. Further, you can travel from the mother ship on small boats through the river's many channels and hike on trails through the forest interior. You'll also have a great place to photograph one of the Amazon's great scenic wonders: the meeting of the Rio Negro and the main Amazon. The black water swirls in whirlpools with the light-colored waters of the master stream, and the top of the boat is a great vantage point to capture this phenomenon.

Several of the hotels in Manaus offer aerial tours of the Amazon, another excellent way to see and photograph the curving patterns of the great river and the surrounding jungle.

Nearby location: Lençóis Maranhenses National Park, in northeastern Brazil, offers a combination of snow-white sand dunes and blue-green freshwater that is unique in the world. During the rainy season, huge amounts of fresh water are captured in beautiful small lakes inside the dunes. Often aquamarine, blue, and deep green during the day, they become wonderful reflecting ponds at sunrise and sunset. The combination of dune patterns and water offers infinite possibilities. Perhaps most amazing is a flight over the park to photograph the patterns of water and sand, a phantasm of form and color. May to September—after the rainy season—is the best time to visit for maximum water in the dunes.

❖ ❖ ❖

Paradise Bay, Antarctic Peninsula

ANTARCTICA

Natural arches in an iceberg

Antarctica

Antarctica is a very different world. The difficulty and expense of getting there will not be undertaken by most people. But since our subject is the entire planet, it would not do to skip a whole continent—especially one with such singular landscapes. Most photographers who visit hope to shoot bird life there, especially penguins. Therefore, shooting landscapes has mostly been done by bird photographers as they travel. One exception is the great book on the landscapes of Antarctica by my hero—one of the founders of landscape photography—Eliot Porter. An inspiration to me because of his great photography and because of his many forays to foreign lands, Porter visited Antarctica with his 4x5 camera in the 1980's. I can't even begin to fathom the difficulties of using this camera in a place like the great southern continent. A used copy of the book called Antarctica can be obtained easily online.

The general public gets to Antarctica by boat from South America, and the storm-tossed seas of the Drake Passage is a formidable barrier to travelers. The Southern Ocean has a deserved reputation for creating havoc with even large boats. Many people, felled by sea sickness, don't get out of bed for days. On other trips, a lucky few find the Passage mercifully calm. It's difficult to know beforehand what you'll experience. On my trip, about two-thirds of the voyagers disappeared to their sickbeds during this period, and a large cruise ship was heavily damaged on its return trip to South America while I was there. Sometimes the predicted storms are expected to be so bad the trips are postponed for days, so be prepared for anything.

All boats are headed for the Antarctic Peninsula, a giant hook of land that is an extension of the Andes Mountains. This is fortunately the most beautiful part of the continent that humans (outside of expeditions) can even hope to visit. The other good news is that once in the fiords and islands of the Peninsula, the winds die down, most people feel better, and the pain of the journey is forgotten. Cameras appear and life returns to a semblance of normal.

Ice patterns in Pleneau Bay

Travelers have their pick of larger cruise ships which offer more creature comforts, or smaller ones that easily penetrate the maze of glacier-covered peaks and plateaus of the area. In either case, pick the most reputable tour you can find. Your life may depend on it.

In Antarctica you will be doing two types of landscape photography: grab-shots of glacial ice and landscapes from a landing boat or the main ship, and land-based shooting with a tripod once you have gone ashore. A waterproof case or pack for your camera gear should go with you all the time. For shore landings, a small waterproof bag to keep clothing layers and other personal items dry is a good idea. Although I thought the weather was almost balmy most of the time,

The Seven Sisters and ocean ice

it can change to a raging blizzard in a moment. Sometimes shore landings are cancelled for weather and other issues.

I believe the three best opportunities for landscape photography in the Antarctic Peninsula are Paradise Bay, The Lemaire Channel, and the Antarctic Sound. It would be important to make sure your boat is spending some time in each of these places, and most of your best opportunities will come from photography done from the ship and not the shore.

Paradise is not a descriptor commonly associated with Antarctica, but if the sun is out, or you happen to be at Paradise Bay during the long hours of sunrise and sunset, the name will make sense to you. Reached by a magnificent fjord with dozens of glaciers tumbling down every slope, and with peaks like giant ice castles, this location is my favorite. The best shots may come from your boat with ice shards and floating icebergs providing great foreground. Paradise Bay has 360 degree views of grandeur, so moving from one side of your ship to the other will pay off.

The icebergs of all sizes calved from Antarctic glaciers in the Antarctic Sound provide the landscape photographer with an endless supply of patterns, shapes, arches, grottoes and huge monuments carved in ice. Shades of blue dominate the color palette here, with some greens and blue-greens thrown in. The blues seem just as strong and colorful on cloudy days as in bright sun. Our boat passed by a typically beautiful berg in the Antarctic Sound with double arches like the ones in Arches National Park made of stone. You will most likely be shooting the ice from a boat, either the main ship or Zodiacs which can whip around through

Lichen on boulder, Half Moon Bay

Left: Paradise Bay

Iceberg in Antarctic Sound

the bergs and reveal their icy secrets.

Sometimes bergs wash up on shore, and can become wonderful subjects there.

The Lemaire Channel is famous for its beauty. At its entrance, if you are lucky, you may be able to get a magnificent sunrise or early morning shot with giant spiky peaks reminiscent of the Torres del Paine in Patagonia. Ideally, your boat would anchor near the entrance to the channel the night before. You would then need to rise at four in the morning to capture the shot. Once inside the Channel, the narrow fjord is surrounded on both sides with towering cliffs that provide great subjects. Also, shooting back out to the mouth of the channel at the surreal entrance pinnacles and the walled-in canyon is a great scene at any time of day.

❖ ❖ ❖

About the Author

Tom Till is one of America's most published photographers. Over 250,000 of his images have appeared in print since 1977. In 1998, Till opened the Tom Till Gallery in Moab, Utah. Till's images depict landscape, nature, history, and travel subjects worldwide, including all fifty states and nearly sixty countries overseas.

Till's stock photography images have been featured by National Geographic Magazine, The New York Times, Outside Magazine, Canon Copiers, Delta Airlines, The New Yorker Magazine, Life Magazine, Browntrout Calendars, Eastman Kodak, Reader's Digest, Rand McNally, MGM, Arizona Highways, Lonely Planet, and thousands of others. Three of Till's images have been used on U.S. postage stamps

An exhibit of his images of UNESCO World Heritage Sites has been traveling the world for almost four years, with stops in Paris, Brussels, Copenhagen, Geneva and Oslo, among others.

Though Till has been know as a master of the large format (4x5) camera and film for over 30 years, he has switched to 35mm digital equipment. Till has one of the largest photo libraries in existence of the Four Corners region.

Profiles about Till have appeared in Backpacker Magazine, Outdoor Photographer Magazine, Camera & Darkroom Magazine, and many other publications. Outdoor Photographer Magazine called him one of the "Lords of Landscape Photography." Also numerous conservation and environmental groups have used Till's photos to galvanize support and illustrate their publications. Till was awarded Arizona Highways Photographer of the Year in 1996, the NANPA/Guilfoyle award for landscape photography in 1994, and was named one of the ten best landscape photographers by Nature's Best Magazine. Till received special awards from The Nature Conservancy in 1998, and 2011. In 2006, Till was awarded the prestigious NANPA Fellow Award for 20 years of excellence in nature photography—one of only a few landscape photographers to receive the honor, and the only Utahan. Till was also featured in the book "World's Best Photographers: Landscape", and he is also the sole photographer for over 30 books. A resident of Moab, Utah for almost 40 years, Till has two grown children, Mikenna Clokey and Bryce Till.

When not photographing, Till is a fan of popular music stretching from the Beach Boys to the Foo Fighters, and movies of all kinds. In 2006, Till was inducted into the Iowa Rock & Roll Hall of Fame. He is a huge devotee of the television show Lost. A voracious reader, Till loves books about music, astronomy, cosmology, and quantum physics.

Tom Till would like to thank his family for their patience in his absences over the twenty five years it took to research and shoot this book, and Laurent Martrès and staff for their advice, input, and additions to the project. Till would especially like to thank his many guides around the world, too numerous to mention, for their help and kindness.

Other titles in the series

Photographing the Southwest: Volume 1 (2nd Ed.)
A guide to the natural landmarks of Southern Utah
by Laurent Martrès
320 pages
ISBN 978-0-916189-12-9

Photographing the Southwest: Volume 2 - Arizona (2nd Ed.)
A guide to the natural landmarks of Arizona
by Laurent Martrès
272 pages
ISBN 978-0-916189-13-6

Photographing the Southwest: Volume 3 (2nd Ed.)
A guide to the natural landmarks of Colorado & New Mexicooregon cover
by Laurent Martrès
272 pages
ISBN 978-0-916189-14-3

Photographing Oregon
A guide to the natural landmarks of Oregon
by Greg Vaughn
304 pages
ISBN 978-0-916189-18-1

Photographing Washington
A guide to the natural landmarks of Washington State
by Greg Vaughn
ISBN 978-0-916189-19-8
Available late 2012

Photographing California: Volume 1 - North
A guide to the natural landmarks of the Golden State
by Gary Crabbe
ISBN 978-0-916189-20-4
Available late 2012

Photographing California: Volume 2 - South
A guide to the natural landmarks of the Golden State
by Jeff Sullivan
ISBN 978-0-916189-21-1
Available 2013